Ruthless Interactions

Jorge Argibay

Published by Jorge Argibay, 2023.

While every precaution has been taken in the preparation of this book, the publisher assumes no responsibility for errors or omissions, or for damages resulting from the use of the information contained herein.

RUTHLESS INTERACTIONS

First edition. October 6, 2023.

ISBN: 979-8223600459

Written by Jorge Argibay.

Table of Contents

Nous savons, en effet, que le salut des hommes est peut-être impossible, mais nous disons que ce n´est pas une raison pour cesser de le tenter et nous disons surtout qu´il n´est pas permis de le dire impossible avant d´avoir fait une bonne fois ce qu´il fallait pour démontrer qu´il ne l´était pas.

CAMUS, Albert [1950] [p.51].

Defining Terms

Interpretation: The production of an interpretation from one spoken or signed language into another that is functionally equivalent and meaningful for all participants.

Consecutive Interpreting: The process whereby the speaker or signer has completed one or more ideas in the source language and pauses while the interpreter transmits that information. This results in a very high standard of accuracy in the interpretation's content.

NHS: National Health Service (NHS), in Great Britain, a comprehensive public-health service under government administration, established by the National Health Service Act of 1946 and subsequent legislation. Virtually the entire population is covered, and health services are free except for certain minor charges.

Middle: Area that was established for administration by the Normans, in many cases based on earlier kingdoms and shires created by the Angles, Saxons, Jutes, Celts and others.

The British Psychological Society (BPS). The British Psychological Society (BPS) is a representative body for psychologists and psychology in the United Kingdom. Guide for Clinicians: Working with Interpreters in Healthcare Settings.

The Australian Psychological Society (APS). The Australian Psychological Society (APS) is the peak body for psychology in Australia. Working with Interpreters: A Practice Guide for Psychologists. The APS has more than 27,000 members, making it the largest professional body representing psychologists in Australia.

To avoid repetition or redundancy in the narrative, these acronyms have been used:

IT- Interpreter.

DT- Doctor (Specialist, Psychologist, Social worker, or others).

PA- The Individual Patient.

APS- Australian Psychological Society.

BPS- British Psychological Society.

Ruthless Interactions is devoted exclusively to the topic of face-to-face interpretive variation and mediumship in the medical and social context.

The relevance of face-to-face interpretation is often preferable to other options, as it enhances the chance of establishing the rapport in a psychotherapy session. It provides a more personal approach, relevant to more complex and detailed issues, which are likely to be dealt with in a counselling context. There is more scope for human interaction and access to visual cues in the session.

Interpreting is a highly specialised skill that involves the accurate, effective and timely translation of information from one language to another. Including an interpreter in the psychology setting may be beneficial when the client prefers to speak, or speaks more fluently, in a language other than the psychologist's primary language, or when the patient's English language skills are deemed inadequate for the consultation.

It is impossible to provide a high quality psychological service without effective communication between the psychologist and the patient. Hence the extreme value of the work of interpreting and the intrinsic value that must be developed, an interaction that does not allow for easy descriptions, it is vital to offer quick, direct, ingenious and, of course, original verbal solutions.

The independence of emotions, theoretical knowledge and preparatory programmes must be put aside in the memory of a mind that needs maximum concentration.

This appreciation of the role works best when the interpreter is accepted as a member of the triadic relationship that has as its common goal the well-being of the patient, and in which each party is accepted for his or her respective source of power or capacity. The provider offers both technical and therapeutic expertise, providing the knowledge and skills the patient needs to achieve their health-related goals.

The patient brings to the encounter their knowledge of their own symptoms, beliefs, needs and expectations, as well as their ultimate right to make decisions for themselves.

The interpreter's expertise lies in his or her linguistic knowledge and understanding of the process of interpreter-assisted communication. His or her commitment is to support both parties in negotiating their respective areas of competence.

The interpreter does not control the content of the messages, but is aware that shared meaning does not occur automatically even if the interlocutors use the same language.

All the sessions referred to are real cases that I have attended as an interpreter (always face-to-face). The real names of the patients are never used, instead, I will mention PA (patient) and a number, e.g. patient PA-22. Patients will remain completely anonymous. I will also not use any date or time of the session (if there is one, it will be fictitious).

There were about 800 visits to medical or social centres in the Middle area. All of them were carried out in the period between October 2018 and January 2020.

To access the appointments I collaborated with several agencies, although there were mainly two, with which I managed 80% of the total number of visits made. The source language was English and the target languages were Spanish, Portuguese and French.

This is not a professional analysis of illnesses, nor is it a pharmaceutical compendium of medications, nor is it a research work, I am only referring to situations that were the result of my interpreting work, at that moment of interaction between psychologist and patient.

At times with personal feedback, at others with comments summarising or assessing the ideas of those present at each session. It is the mirror of the need for linguistic help as a transposition of the emotional need to help the patient and, for his resentment, the compact package of mixed feelings that surrounds such sessions.

The illnesses reported, suffered by the patients are in common (with exceptions), some of them have an impact on today's society wherever we are in the world, although my cases are located in the aforementioned Middle.

There will be no bibliographical references, I always refer to real cases with illnesses that are sometimes told in a generic context, following the pattern of influence on the patient in interest. Mention will be made of the British Psichology Society (BPS) and the Australian Psichology Society (APS) on issues related to the field of interpretation. The pictures were captured from gettyimages.

1. What's Going on Inside my Brain?

PA-88.

It was clear, with a few IT visits for mental health cases, I could express how the diagnosis was arrived at. In other words, the question would be:

How are mental disorders diagnosed?. The steps to obtain a diagnosis would include:

- A medical history.

- A physical examination and eventually laboratory tests, if the professional considers that other medical conditions may be causing the symptoms.

- A psychological evaluation. It will answer questions about thinking, feelings and behaviour.

The appointment started at 14.00pm. It was at the Centre for Mental Health. This hospital is a 110-bed independent private psychiatric hospital providing life-changing care for adults aged 18 and over.

The record did not contain any data from PA-88. Mental health cases adhere to a comprehensive PA privacy protocol. I submitted my details at the front desk and was told to go up to the first floor. The atmosphere was cold, empty corridors and sounds in the distance.

Nobody in the corridor, unlike in some hospitals in Mental Health Centres there is always an atmosphere of loneliness, of doubt, of absence of staff. Very quiet, so I decided to take the stairs instead of the lift.

When I attend such cases, I just try to relax, that's all, it doesn't cross my mind what kind of case it will be or who the patient will be. On the first floor there was another small desk, and I showed my chart again with my schedule and details. I was invited to go through the security door and a nurse, without so much as a word, kindly pointed out the room where I was to perform my task.

It was about 5 minutes before 14.00pm when I entered the room and, to my surprise, there were quite a few people there waiting for me. Around a large table, there was a group of people who were supposed to be expecting me to start the meeting. They all looked at me as I approached. Nobody said anything particularly noticeable.

I was seated next to a staff member, who pointed out to me the issues to be discussed in the agenda of the meeting. The most important one was that it had to be made very clear to the patient exactly when he would have to leave the hospital.

At first it was a little difficult for me to understand this question, as I usually attend therapy meetings, but I had never attended a session oriented to communicate, let's say, the patient's discharge from the centre. After asking the counsellor what was the reason for this situation, she told me that it was because she had set an initial discharge date for a few days before and the patient had refused to leave.

An IT had been called in to facilitate the meeting in generally, but also to clarify this particular issue. The fact that he had refused to leave explained why there was such a large group of attendees. They were not introduced, I mean from the first moment I arrived, I had to find out which position they had according to the explanation they were giving. Others were simply observers, but without intervening.

Given the presentation, the atmosphere was one of a rather complex or at least problematic case. I assume that informing a PA that he has to leave and that he refuses to do so has its degree of internal severity, although I don't know how or what kind of measures are implemented in these cases.

Indeed, PA-88 was present and very close to me. He was young, I figure about 25 years old, wearing a kind of housecoat with pyjamas, and he had the face of someone who has just got up, rather forlorn and with dark circles under his eyes.

He was quiet, observing his surroundings, with his hands folded on his two legs. He stared at me and asked me if I was IT. I nodded. He didn't say anything, he just went back to his initial position.

No one introduced me to the attendees, they just started as soon as they saw we were all there. There was an introductory speech, so for the moment I had to translate in front of PA-88. The person next to me pointed out that I could take it easy because that briefing contained details that the young man already knew about his internment, motives and the disease of diagnosis.

That I could be calm and wait, because the young man was apparently able to understand some English. My work would be focusing on telling him that he could not fail again, that he could not overstay his welcome at the Centre, that he would have to leave on the date that would be specified.

He urged me to please raise this issue and to do it face to face with patient-88. For now the facts were substantial, but not crucial to the motive that had brought us there. Let's get to the facts," said one of the women present.

The young man had been diagnosed with Obsessive Compulsive Disorder (OCD). Meanwhile, the review went on, to which everyone listened very attentively. The other member of the group on my left, a woman, made some quiet explanations about the illness. I was not instructed to translate these details, they were just a slight, very slight remark.

Experiencing a mental health problem is often upsetting, confusing and frightening, especially at the beginning. If you feel unwell, you may think it is a sign of weakness or that you are 'losing your mind'.

These fears are often enhanced by the negative (often unrealistic) way in which people with mental health problems are portrayed in the usual environment. This can inhibit you from talking about your troubles or seeking help. This, in turn, can increase their distress and sense of isolation. This is why PA-88 came to us, he required help (said the speaker).

However, not everyone finds it helpful to think of their mental health in this way. It depends on your traditions and beliefs, and you may have different ideas about the best way to deal with the circumstances. In many cultures, emotional well-being is closely associated with religious or spiritual life. And difficult experiences may be just one part of how you understand your overall identity.

Following her overview, she gave a further definition of OCD:

Obsessive-compulsive disorder (OCD) is a frequent, chronic and long-lasting disorder in which a person has uncontrollable and recurrent thoughts (obsessions) and/or behaviours (compulsions) that they feel the urge to repeat over and over again.

It was to be assumed that the audience knew what was being talked about, although no one made any gestures or reactions. PA-88 was still listening (I wonder if his mind was really with us in the room or somewhere else).

In his phases PA-88 was constantly scratching, as mentioned below, which was one of the usual symptoms of the disease. The affected areas were eventually damaged. This question was further investigated.

A person with excoriation (skin picking) disorder, repeatedly picks at their own skin enough to cause injury. The skin picking behaviour causes significant distress or difficulty in work, social interactions or other activities.

It can trigger feelings of loss of control, shame and embarrassment and may lead to avoidance of social relationships. Individuals with excoriation disorder have often made repeated attempts to decrease or stop skin picking. The PA has significantly decreased it.

The behaviour may be triggered by feelings of anxiety or boredom. It may be preceded by a growing sense of tension and lead to a sense of relief afterwards, or it may be a more automatic behaviour. It may sometimes involve a drive to try to fix perceived imperfections.

Obsessions are recurrent and pervasive thoughts, impulses or images that are provoking distressing emotions such as anxiety, fear or anger. Many people with OCD realise that they are a manifestation of their mind and that they are extreme or irrational. However, the distress caused by these intrusive thoughts cannot be cleared up by logic or reasoning.

Most people with OCD try to de-escalate the distress of obsessive thoughts, or undo perceived threats, through the use of compulsions. They may also try to disregard or suppress the obsessions or distract themselves with other activities. PA-88 had received appropriate treatment and medication.

Examples of typical content of obsessive thoughts from PA-88:

- Fear of contamination by people or the environment.

- Fear of committing aggression or being harmed (self or loved ones).

- Extreme concern that something is not complete.

PA-88 had also been undergoing Cognitive Behavioural Therapy (CBT), known as exposure and response prevention (ERP). During treatment sessions, PA-88 is exposed to feared situations or images that focus on his obsessions. Initially, the treatment resulted in increased anxiety.

The patient has been trained to avoid performing his usual compulsive behaviours (known as response prevention). By simply staying in a feared situation without anything terrible happening, the patient learns that his fearful memories are just thoughts.

PA-88 was sitting between these two people facing me, kind of in a circle, he didn't have his independent access to the table. It was clear that they only wanted me to focus on the translation, facing PA-88, whatever he said didn't seem to matter, I mean, it was all posed as him having to nod, little else.

In fact, the very few things he said were translated to the person to my left, who seemed to be the one in charge, although he didn't introduce

himself either, nobody introduced himself, I mean, nobody told me
what function he had or suchlike. It was all very suspenseful.

The mother had been the one to request his admission to the centre
(due to the risk of self-harm) in the anticipation of support for her son.
He had been receiving a variety of care during his time in this hospital,
both social and educational help to deal with his disorder. On the other
hand, he had received medication (six to 12 weeks, mentioned by the
doctor as the standard period of response of the PA to treatment).

Treatment is based on the mental disorder the PA suffers from and
its acuity. The mother and doctors have worked out a tailor-made
treatment plan for her son. It usually entailed some level of therapy. It
also included taking medication.

The mother, after subsequent consultation with the doctors, had
agreed that basic care or treatment was not enough, and she was also
afraid of assault, which is why she applied for admission to the
psychiatric centre. The doctors had told her that in some cases, more
in-depth treatment may be considered necessary. It may be necessary to
go to a psychiatric hospital.

It may be because your mental illness is grave, or because you are at risk of harming yourself or someone else. In the hospital you would receive counselling, can always talk in a group and do activities with mental health professionals and other patients. The mother had agreed to this option after listening to the counselling.

PA-88 was quiet, his hands folded, he barely gestured and did not move. Only his eyes were turning towards me, to withdraw them at once, but for the moment he did not mention anything to me. I had the feeling that before my arrival, they had briefed him on how the meeting was going to be and, maybe that's why he was relaxed, or maybe because he didn't care about what was going on there.

For a moment as I listened, I wondered to myself why PA-88's mother was not in attendance. As if she could hear my thoughts, shortly afterwards the woman on the left told me that a written copy had been forwarded to the postal address of the mother, who had been absent from Middle for personal reasons in recent days.

The Centre agreed that PA-88 was already much better, was recovered and that he had to leave the Centre on the appointed date (there were a few days of extension left). I had to repeat this to PA-88 several times, I kept repeating the day and date, which were also written on a document that we could see in front of us (the same one that had been sent to his mother).

PA-88 nodded sharply, said very good, very good and then repeated the day and date. That seemed to reassure those present, who looked at the affected person for acceptance.

Everything seemed in place and very clear. The meeting had been very satisfactory, or so it seemed to me. PA-88 thanked me, let me see a soft smile and told me that he didn't really feel like going anywhere and that his mother was the only thing he had and that what bothered him the most were the shots.

PA-88: those damn jabs, they're going to destroy me, I already told my mother not to inject me any more, but nobody listens to me and they've started giving them again, they've left me totally stranded, he told me.

The meeting was over, I had been told I could leave. I left avoiding further contact with the patient.

I was left with a feeling of certain uneasiness, I would have liked PA-88 to have spoken more, to have mentioned something about the illness, to have acknowledged his progress, or at least to have spoken to those present on more occasions.

I don't know, maybe it was the protocol for these cases, or maybe he was also tired and would rather not participate, given that the reason for the meeting was very concrete. It would also have been nice if his mother had been present, since it seemed that it was her decision to confine him to the hospital.

I have tried to assess for myself the interpersonal dynamic situations. The presence of an interpreter can alter the dynamics of the therapeutic relationship between the psychologist and the PA. Transference and Counter-transference reactions can be complex. Potential areas of concern may include:

- The PA and interpreter form an alliance that excludes the psychologist.
- The interpreter and psychologist form an alliance that excludes the PA; or
- Rejection of the interpreter by the PA (or psychologist).

A psychologist who is working with an interpreter should be aware of these scenarios and must consider the consequences of working with an interpreter. The best practice for managing changes in interpersonal dynamics is to reflect on them with the interpreter and to use peer consultation.

If the psychologist finds that the interpreter has not connected with the AP or is not coping with the content of the sessions, it may be advisable to reconsider seeking an alternative interpreter.

I had done my best to cope with the substance of the meeting. The result was very good, the most important points were clarified and the communication was smooth.

We would say that PA-88, as far as we could judge from his condition, had improved in matters of:

- He had lost the fear of causing harm to himself or to another person by not being careful enough or by acting on a violent impulse.

- The non-need for constant reassurance.

- As far as medicines were concerned, it was evident that shots of whatever kind did not seem to have been satisfying, although their positive contribution to his improvement seemed unquestionable.

******

PA-55.

The DT on this occasion did make me an initial briefing and reminded me of the Code of Ethics, by which psychologists who use interpreters must comply with:

(a) take reasonable steps to ensure that interpreters are competent to work as interpreters in the relevant context.

(b) take reasonable steps to ensure that the interpreter does not have a multiple relationship with the client that may impair their judgement.

(c) take reasonable steps to ensure that the interpreter is aware of any other relevant provisions of this Code.

(d) Obtain the client's informed consent to use the selected interpreter. The DT told me that the agency had told her of my worth and that she was glad that I was able to assist at the meeting and that she was pleased with my support.

The session begun very powerfully, the PA-55 sitting next to me, telling me to translate, in an impulsive way. She was asking the doctor how she had changed her appointment. She was quite confrontational in expressing herself, the doctor did not seem impressed (for me it was the first time with this patient).

She said that she was fed up with the therapy and that she might not come back. She said that she liked doing harm, that it was no big deal.

She had been an in-patient in the psychiatric hospital and now she was attending follow-up sessions here in this private centre since she had left the hospital. the problem was that she was relapsing in the self-aggressions.

To my considerable surprise, she showed her arm and, to tell the truth, it had extensive wounds, several cuts, some of them seemed to have been there for quite some time and were almost healed. Some were caused by glass.

The doctor listened and looked into her eyes attentively. I guessed that the patient did not have any special utensils at hand, for our safety.

After a few minutes, the DT assumed a remote approach, and I could see the patient's mood change abruptly. She put both her hands on her face and she began to cry.

The DT told PA-55 not to forget all the talks they had had in the past. He went on to mention his overall assessment of the disease:

Psychosis, including schizophrenia, is characterised by distortions in thinking, perception, emotions, language, sense of self and behaviour. During a psychotic episode, you may experience such things as hallucinations and ravings.

Symptoms: In terms of perception, you may think that other people are talking about you or hear voices. You may also feel sad and angry, or that you are constantly being watched. Behaviourally, you may have difficulty sleeping, talk to yourself and behave offensively.

Treatment and help: Medication is the main form of treatment, as it can help with altered biochemical balances in the brain and relief symptoms such as hallucinations. Psychotherapy can help the person to understand their illness and cope with the impact it has on their life. Rehabilitation and counselling help develop social interaction and independent living skills.

This was a patient with a history of schizophrenia. She had been under treatment for considerable time, then she was no longer in hospital because her behaviour had been improving and she had requested to return to her family as she had some children and, let's not overlook the fact that she was a foreigner (whenever there is an IT it is because there is a foreigner), her visa status became critical.

Being such a delicate case, I did my best to properly liaise between the two parties, no one seemed to complain about it. The situation appeared to be calming down, and I was happy about that.

Now the doctor would divert the conversation and ask PA-55 about the family. She embraced the challenge and answered in short sentences, giving herself plenty of time to react, as if she were talking about the life of someone else's family.

After all, she was probably well enough, because PA-55 came alone to the consulting room, no one was accompanying her. It was clear that she now had complete self-sufficiency in her personal life.

******

PA-46.

PA-46 was diagnosed with Bipolar Disorder. She has lived in denial and isolation at home for a long time. She came to the session in the company of her mother. The aim of these sessions was to focus on psychological support (counselling).

The DT referred to knowing how to recognise the triggers and signs of a depressive or manic episode and psychological treatment, such as talking therapy, which can help her to cope with depression and giving her advice on how to improve her relationships.

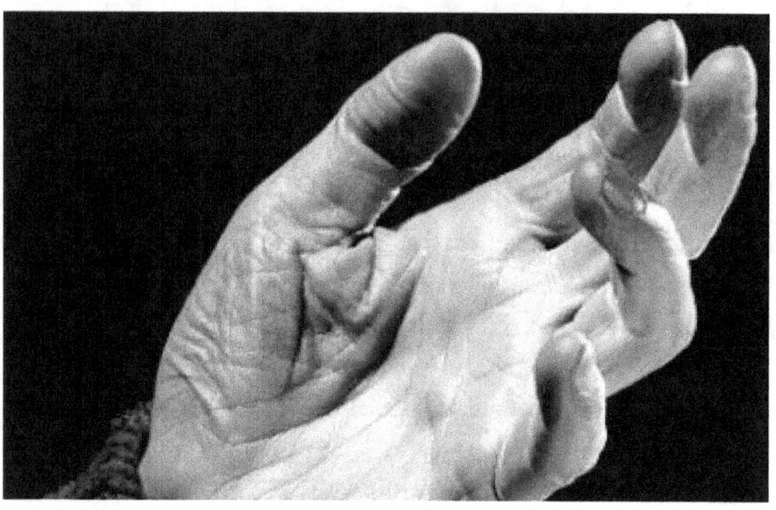

PA-46 had gone through a long period of isolation, due to her hallucinations, intense episodes (although not reported accurately in this session), she had experienced a state of permanent disillusionment, she felt that she was the cause of the harm suffered by people close to her, that she was blocked (psychosis).

She tried to control all these symptoms with psychological help and appropriate treatment (this was the part in which the mother intervened the most).

DT- Treatment aims to stabilise the person's mood and reduce the severity of the symptoms. The aim is to help the person to function effectively in everyday life.

From what I could gather from the dialogue (it was the first time I had attended this case), PA-46 was feeling well and, the mother had reached out to the psychologist, asking for an expert opinion on whether the meds should be withdrawn. This was a very sensitive point, because the symptoms could return.

The mother was worried that her daughter, at her age, could be starting to have enough independency in her life, that she could already be able to realise some personal projects and go all the way to the end.

DT: However, it is unlikely that an inflated state of mind will endure. Even if it does, it may be quite difficult to keep focus or to follow through with plans. This can make it difficult to follow a project through to the end.

Nightmares, constant feelings of fear, states of constant remoteness (self-absorption), lack of concentration, scenes where he imagined himself hurting other people (cutting with knives, squeezing their throats) were some of the sufferings of PA-46.

Once the treatment improves the person's feeling, he or she may stop taking the medication. Then, the symptoms may reappear (this was the psychologist's concern).

The DT believed that it was still a bit premature to stop the meds, and thought they would keep them for a relatively short period of time. She was optimistic about the overall results and considered that the progress of PA-46 was encouraging, although she saw the medication as an undeniable support and to stop it was extremely risky for the time being.

Maintaining the therapy was essential (CBT), although there was an on-line channel that they had not yet used and that they were going to start doing so, to simplify contact with the specialist without having to physically visit the clinic.

DT: We have to be sure to avoid those symptoms of psychosis, including hallucinations, which involve hearing or seeing things that are not there, and delusions, which are false but strongly felt beliefs. We can't run the risk of the curve going into depressive episodes, that would be very dramatic.

Through Cognitive Behavioural Therapy (CBT), the patient can successfully manage triggers:

- recognise and take action to manage key triggers, such as stress.

- identify the early symptoms of an episode and take steps to manage them.

- work on factors that help maintain a stable mood for as long as possible.

- enlist the help of family members, teachers and peers.

- These measures can help the person to maintain positive relationships at home/work.

Bipolar disorder cannot be completely cured, but the treatment focuses on the competent management of acute episodes and the prevention of new episodes. Other variations point to neurotransmitter imbalances, impaired thyroid function, circadian rhythm disturbances and elevated levels of the stress hormone cortisol.

DT: External environmental and psychological factors are also thought to be involved in the development of bipolar disorder. These external factors are called triggers (stress, substance abuse, medication, seasonal changes, sleep deprivation). However, the current episode of bipolar disorder in PA-46 is not associated with an explicit trigger.

DT: Accept your illness, don't be ashamed of it. Keep on with your treatment. From there, regain the self you have lost. I assure you that you will lose yourself. But there is nothing to fear. After all, the whole is in constant evolution. Apart from biological constraints, you can shape it as you wish.

The DT made observations under the heading of medication, already well-known to both parties to preventing episodes of mania and depression, known as mood stabilisers (which she was taking on a daily basis on a prolonged basis) and, the medications to treat the main symptoms of depression and mania when symptoms occur, learning to identify the triggers and signs of a depressive or manic episode, and psychological treatment.

DT: These medications must be maintained to prevent episodes of mania and depression. The mood stabilisers, which you take every day. You have to carry on, of course, I know they come from a long term but that's what it's all about.

Finally, they were reminded of lifestyle advice, to try to exercise regularly, to plan activities that they enjoy and give them a sense of achievement, as well as advice on improving their diet and getting more sleep.

If we were to reverse the patients' wishes, we could say that this is the most favourite disease, I mean, in the sense that it is the most common ailment among the cases I assisted. Many are the PA's who need translation, many are the foreigners living in Middle who experience Diabetes, they are the top one in disease assessment.

PA-19.

PA-19 was from a Central American country, after previous tests today he comes to the doctor relaxed and calmed. He works in some construction industry, he has travelled before to Italy where he has obtained his dual nationality (many PA's talk about this circumstance as very desirable in the geographic environment). As soon as he has savings he travels back and forth to his home country. Comments made while the doctor was taking notes.

The doctor has confirmed all the results, which are not favourable, and the comparative assessment. Of the three results obtained from the test, his result was among the highest, hence the indication of diabetes.

DT: You will have to start taking insulin. It's the beginning of a no-return path.

PA-19: I am going to have to take insulin?.

Doctor: yes, there is no choice, this is already very advanced, as the test result shows.

PA-19: How long will I have to take insulin?.

Doctor: There is no time frame. Your body will be in permanent need of insulin.

DT: An excess of glucose in the blood can cause serious health problems that damage the blood vessels, nerves, heart, eyes and kidneys. It is imperative to fight it straight away to avoid more serious damage.

Type 2 diabetes is usually diagnosed by the glycosylated hemoglobin (A1C) test. This blood test indicates your average blood sugar level over the past two to three months.

DT: Type 2 diabetes occurs when the body does not generate enough insulin or does not consume insulin as it should.

DT: You are overweight. That's a big challenge, too. Weight loss translates into better control of blood sugar, cholesterol, triglycerides and blood pressure. You can start to see improvements in these factors after losing as little as 5% of your body weight.

The more weight you lose, the greater the health benefits. We will set the option of losing up to 15% of your body weight as a goal.

PA: What medication will I have to take?.

DT: In the first instance, diet and exercise will be the best allies. Insulin will be the one that directly fights the disease.

Among the medications, metformin, because it works by reducing the production of glucose in the liver and improving the body's sensitivity to insulin so that it can use it more effectively.

******

PA-20.

PA-20 was in a lot of pain and discomfort, the woman ascribes it to a sedentary lifestyle and that she had gained quite a few pounds. She was over 110K and not quite 5'5" tall.

Diagnosis: Diabetes. Reason for appointment: Recommendations for self-injection syringe use and follow-up therapy. She came with a child (her daughter, about 12 years old).

Symptoms of diabetes: Extreme hunger. Fatigue or drowsiness. Blurred vision.

Slowly healing wounds, sores or bruises. Dry, itchy skin.

The doctor made the point that in his case the diabetes was connected to an alimentary problem, as he was significantly overweight and this was not helpful in combating the disease.

There was something upset in PA-20's look. She described to the doctor daily episodes of her life, assuring her that her diet was not at all bad, that she slept quite well and that there were no major setbacks in her life that made her worry overmuch. She did not comprehend the reason for this illness.

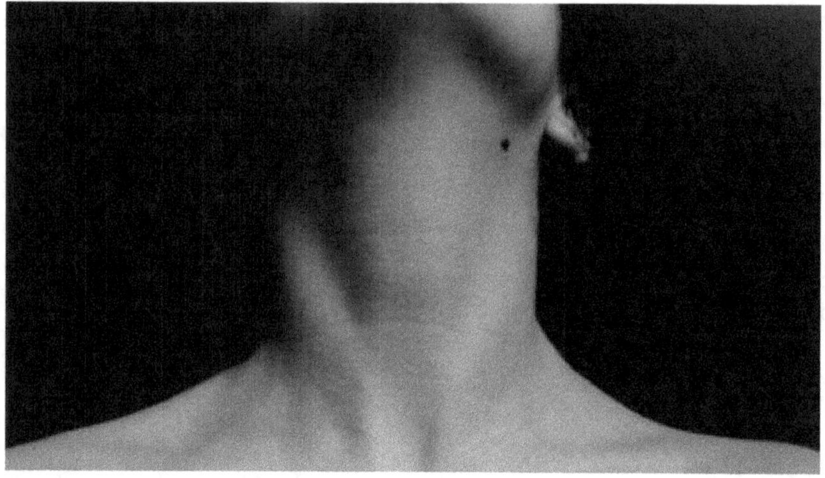

The DT was explaining to her that diabetes is mainly a nutritional problem in her case, because she was very overweight.

The DT explained some risk factors for type 2 diabetes:

- Weight. Obesity is the most important risk factor for type 2 diabetes. The more overweight you are, the more resistant your body is to insulin.

- Age. The risk of type 2 diabetes increases with age, mostly after age 45. While you can't change your age, you can work on other risk factors to reduce it. She was in my 50s so more danger.

- Family history. You can't change your family history, but it's still relevant for you and your doctor to know if diabetes runs in your family. Your risk for diabetes is higher if your mother, father or a sibling has diabetes.

PA-20: Yes, my father had diabetes.

DT: Alcohol and tobacco consumption can increase the risk of type 2 diabetes. Stop smoking as soon as possible.

PA-20: Yes, I have been smoking on a regular basis for years.

We can make changes to reduce the risk significantly. two basic recommendations:

- Exercise and weight control. Exercising and maintaining a healthy weight can reduce the risk of diabetes. Any amount of activity is better than none. Try to exercise 30 to 60 minutes most days of the week.

- A diet high in fat, calories and cholesterol increases the risk. An incorrect diet can lead to obesity (another risk factor for diabetes) and other health problems. A healthy diet is rich in fiber and low in fat, cholesterol, salt and sugar. Also remember to watch your portion sizes. How much you eat is as important as what you eat.

PA-20: Don't tell me that I am going to be on a diet.

DT: Yes, I'm afraid, we will have to guide you in that sense, so that you keep eating what you like, but in regulated portions.

PA-20: But what about my hair?.

DT: What is wrong with your hair?.

PA-20: My God, am I going to lose my hair?.

DT: You mean, is your hair going to fall out of your head?. Have you noticed any symptoms?.

PA-20: No, but I saw a young woman on a TV program who said that her hair had fallen out with diabetes.

DT: Hair loss is often related to diabetes. It is commonly believed that certain problems caused by diabetes can lead to hair loss, amongst them a disorder of the immune system called alopecia areata, poor circulation and hyperglycemia. Insulin is an important hormone that helps cells use blood sugar as a source of energy.

When it is not being produced or used incorrectly, it leads to an increase in blood sugar which, in turn, can lead to multiple serious body-wide complications if it is not properly controlled.

DT: But you say you haven't missed it, right?. That you haven't noticed any symptoms so far, correct?. Then you don't have to worry about it. Good nutrition is what will help us to make sure that we prevent any kind of negative side effects, combined with the right dosage. Stress should be avoided as much as possible.

DT: in responding to your previous comments that your diet is not all bad, I remind you that the food itself is not the issue, what is key in the environment of diabetes, is the quantity, since you can or may eat whatever you want, but it is the quantities that give the value, if before you ate for example in your dinner two bowls of rice with a side dish, now you will have to eat half a bowl of rice.

The volume of food is the *key* in the long term will surely define your evolution with the disease and the signs of improvement in your body.

******

PA-87.

PA had been diagnosed with pre-diabetes, today's appointment was to instruct him on how to use the injector to shoot himself (in the abdominal area) and he would be given his first shot during this session.

PA-87 did not entirely understood in principle why he had to do it, although he would accept the demands, because his family had convinced him, but he felt sure that the deprivation of food, above all, was not for him.

In his opinion, he said, food was very essential, it was part of the correct development of his body and mind, and he had raised his family that way. Pre-diabetes diagnosis. He did not accept his condition easily. Initial struggles to keep him on his pricks.

DT: The condition can be controllable and even reversed by taking diabetes medications and making lifestyle changes. In his case we will start with insulin drips, but in very limited doses. With the help of the IT, I will explain how you can give it yourself, or someone in a family member's home. It is very basic, just follow the procedure.

DT: There are several types of insulin on the market. Each type begins to work at a differing rate, which is known as "onset", and, in what is known as "duration", the time it takes effect also varies. Most types of insulin reach a peak, which is when they have the strongest effect. After the peak, the effects of insulin wear off over the next few hours.

PA-87 was becoming more and more cooperative. He felt that the change in his life habits since he had come to Middle was the real and true cause of the disease, that his lifestyle was much healthier when he lived in his own country. He was explaining his point of view, while the DT was preparing the medical kits.

He was a very kind person, one of the few that before entering the consultation, when he introduced himself to me, he thanked me for being there to help him, because he said that for now his english was very poor.

At home his wife was the one who managed the local language for his needs or when she accompanied him, but today he had preferred not to be with him, both his wife and his daughter, although they supported him 100% and were going to take care of his health.

He said that he did not really felt very fat, yes, he had gained weight, but his overall feeling was not bad, and that eating was agreeable to him, in the sense that he was always in a good mood and, above all, because gaining weight did not deprive him of agility or activity in his life.

He was a businessman, or at least the way he used to talk was that of a man who was very accustomed to the business world. He was explaining that his professional life had also changed a bit when he came to this country.

He was referring to the fact that (presumably) they had left their country due to political reasons (I don't know exactly what) and that their status there was very favourable, but in Middle they had to start from scratch and, well, he thought that there could also be a degree of guilt in their new life habits and climate, which, by the way, was much colder and more harsh.

The DT was not very keen to follow this reasoning (they had already had a previous session) and today she wanted to focus on the main topic of instructing on how to use the injector to initiate the shooting. The DT looked at me and told me to repeat this point, because knowing how to handle it was essential, although it was easy, at the beginning, she knew from her own previous experience, that many people did not use it well and of course, if it was not handled correctly, it would be prejudicial to the treatment. It was essential to fix this aspect of today's session.

PA-87 continued with his own analysis, making various remarks. There was a good connection (with the IT), he was a very straightforward and direct person in what he said, and he smelled very good, it must be said, from the moment he entered the room, the smell of his perfume permeated the atmosphere of the room.

I had never met a patient who gave off such a strong and pleasant aroma. If it were not for my work and upbringing, I would have asked him what brand he used, and the quantity he used, because we could smell it from far away, guessing his presence.

But as this question is not a major priority, let's go back to what concerns us. The direct instruction on how to use the injector came. Today he would be injected for the first time while at the same time explaining how he would have to do it at home in the future.

DT: This is an injector. An insulin injector is pretty much like a writing pen, but the tip is a needle, as you can see (showing him the injector). Some insulin injectors come filled with insulin and are disposable. These have space for an insulin cartridge that is inserted and replaced after use.

Insulin injectors are easier to use than syringes and needles. Each type of injector has different features that can help with injections. This reusable injector has a memory function, which can remember the dose amounts and timing of each injection.

******

PA-77.

The session was aimed at letting the PA-77 (diabetes patient) know how to utilize the electronic devices at home (self-monitoring), how to do it and when he will have to report back to the clinic with the results. It was indeed a critical issue for the follow-up of the disease and its progression or treatment.

DT: Individual risk perception could be enhanced by using supplementary blood pressure measurements taken outside the clinical setting, such as home or ambulatory readings. Home blood pressure readings contribute between one-third and one-half of the ambulatory reading.

DT: By providing an inexpensive and convenient method to increase the number of readings, home monitoring has the potential to reduce the error in assessing the patient's current blood pressure, which is likely to be high if only a few clinical readings are used.

PA-77 was an adult man, around 65 years old, with a fragile health aspect. He barely spoke, listened to the DT's guidance, my translations, then nodded and waited for the practical steps that would help him to do a correct follow-up at home, as it was the first time he would do the self-monitoring.

How often should readings be taken?. It is desirable to take readings both in the morning and at night, both to detect diurnal fluctuations in blood pressure in the untreated state and to assess the adjustment of treatment in patients taking medication.

The optimization would be to take three consecutive readings in the morning and three in the evening on 3 days a week for at least 2 weeks. It would also be useful to obtain some readings on weekend days. The physician did not provide a form to the patient, as this device will store all the data and the physician will be able to check the results.

The physician explained (in its generality) N-of-1 trials to determine the optimal treatment. One possible way to improve hypertension control with the drugs available for treatment is to use home monitoring to conduct "N-of-1" trials, in which each patient receives a number of different drugs administered in a sequential pattern.

DT: Because individual drugs vary in the time required to achieve their full effect on blood pressure, it is likely that a minimum of 3 weeks would be needed to test each drug.

The application of self-monitoring using electronic devices for routine assessment of hypertensive BP is likely to provide worthwhile variables and streamline monitoring of the disease (without having to make periodic clinic visits).

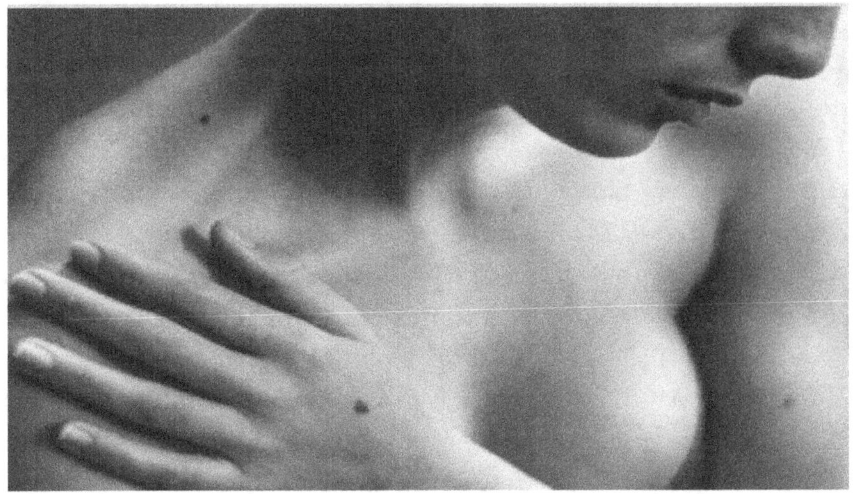

We will start with metformin tablets, which also come in liquid form. Metformin helps the liver to produce less glucose and the body to make better use of insulin. This medication may help you lose a small amount of weight.

Other oral drugs work in different ways to lower blood glucose levels. Combining two or three types of diabetes medicine can lower blood glucose levels more effectively than taking just one medicine. We will pursue this line of work.

The doctor got up and outlined the steps to be followed to PA-77, who had already started to install the device in the patient's body, who should go home with it in place and keep it for the opportune follow-up.

The explanations were given, the PA now seemed more confident about how to use the device and the session came to an end, with the basic purpose accomplished with the assistance of the IT.

To conclude, here are some theoretical indications that the doctor pronounced before the final closing:

DT: Blood pressure during the day is also impacted by emotional state, as most feelings raise both systolic and diastolic blood pressure to some extent. Affective state may also shape the blood pressure of men/ women in professional occupations differently from that of men in non-professional jobs.

DT: Increased dietary salt has also been observed to increase mean daily ambulatory blood pressure. However, the amount of salt in the diet may affect the activity-dependent variance of blood pressure during the day. Thus, factors such as gender, time of year, diet, and social class should be taken into account when assessing ambulatory blood pressure measurements for pathology.

The doctor even drew up indicative tables based on follow-up studies with some of her long-standing patients. Obviously, the DT gave explicit instructions for the use of the PA-77.

In order to have a suitable control of this disease, a constant self-monitoring of the glycemia (blood sugar level) and blood pressure variables must be performed through standardized methodologies such as the glucometer and the commercial blood pressure monitor.

The device incorporates a diary that allows the user to keep a manual record of each measurement taken. The device carries a data memory which is downloaded to a computer using dedicated proprietary software associated with the medical equipment in place.

PA-77 also asked some very quick questions:

How often should I check my blood sugar?. What do these numbers means?. Are there patterns that will show I need to change my diabetes treatment?. What changes are needed in the future to my diabetes health care plan?.

DT: Never forget that monitoring your blood sugar regularly is the most pivotal thing you can do to self-manage your diabetes.

DT streamlined her answers and diverted them to the glucometer utilization. PA-77 was confident with the replies.

******

PA-80.

There were many diabetes patients who, after appointments for the most basic follow-up and monitoring and prevention of the disease, were referred to dietary specialists.

The follow-up was very straight forward, i.e., questions referring to the daily menus of the PA-80, descriptive notes from the DT, for follow-up at follow-up visits, and advice or recommendations for changes to be made in her daily diet.

DT: We are going to structure the meals by days. If you don't remember a menu, that's fine. The goal is to determine your most obvious eating habits and to establish in substance the ingredients that should be avoided in your diet.

PA-80: That is fine.

DT: Let's start. What did you consume on Monday, for breakfast, lunch and dinner.

The query would be reiterated for the seven days of the week. The DT wrote down all the comments, sauces, breakfast, coffee, tea, everything that was said was worthy. Everything that was being said had relevance and was pertinent from a dietary and control point of view for the coming months.

PA-80 seemed to have a pattern of repetitive and consistent meals at least three days a week, including Saturdays and Sundays, where her family always had about the same thing to eat. I figured it was a cultural factor.

The complementary food for the midday meals for almost 90% of the days was rice. From the beginning, the DT emphasized the significance of this ingredient, contrary to the PA-80 who saw it as irrelevant, that is to say, it was their routine to make use of it in their meals.

The DT also wanted further details as to the type of rice they ate, if it was from a certain country, if it was white or brown, if there were other varieties, and how it was cooked. With spices, alone, how it was cooked, if it was mixed with other ingredients, or of course, the quantity of salt or other add-ons. She requested and demanded everything in detail.

The DT was quite young, about 35, her hair was tied back, and she wore a flowered dress that offered her a very professional look, she inspired trust in her queries, security in the way she handled the talk. You could tell she knew what she was doing, where she was going with her research and the desired results she wanted to achieve.

PA-80 acknowledged that she put a lot of rice on the table at lunch and dinner. She ate a lot and always kept repeating. She commented with an air of conviction, that is, as if she assumed that everyone did the same thing, as if she could not conceive of any other way to accompany her food. It was self-evident that this dish had been a regular in her diet for a long time.

The DT said that this was a very important aspect, that we would come back to it, but that to go into more detail, she would have to stop consuming rice. PA-80 leaned back in her chair (she was sitting in front of me) and sighed in disbelief. It was as if the DT had punched her in the stomach (figuratively speaking of course).

The DT noticed the circumstance and softened her comment instantly: DT- Don't worry dear lady, I don't mean that I am going to forbid you to eat rice forever, what I mean is that you are going to have to reduce the quantity of rice you eat on a regular basis.

Don't worry, you will be able to continue taking rice and eating it often, but I do need, and your body requires you to control the dosage, it's not about eliminating it, it's about keeping control of the quantity of rice you eat.

For example, if you had three portions at lunch and two at dinner, now you will have to have one portion at lunch and one portion at dinner.

We have to reduce the quantity ingested gradually, until in a prudentially short time, you feel comfortable taking that food that you like but in a very reduced quantity. This will be repeated also with other foods that can affect your health.

We proceeded with the descriptions of the proposed menus of the PA-80. There was a bit of everything, one could say, that they had fairly well-balanced eating habits, mostly centered on meat. There was little fish and a lot of precooked food that went into the microwave. The PA seemed happy talking about menus, I sensed that she liked to cook.

DT: Look, this is the book that I am going to suggest as a reference, about menus for diabetics. We strongly recommend it to all PA's that come with these diabetic disorders, it is really good, huge diversity of menus and the right quantity to take, it includes pictures.

Obviously, when you make a menu that does not appear here you should simply let yourself be guided by a similar one. The idea is to keep the quantity under control.

There was a subject that some DT's had previously told me and, at the same time, that I had observed in these cases, the relevance of the PA telling the truth when talking about his food, not lying with the menus, otherwise, he could not be followed up correctly.

It was a complex issue anyway, the DT's were always suspicious of the veracity of the info, particularly from the PA's who were attending for the first time, it was allegedly a question of initial trust.

She would eat a lot of meat, she said, especially the typical pork fried steak, sometimes with beef (red meat). She used to eat a lot of pasta in the evenings with a mixture of sauces. She always had at least two dishes.

On Fridays they ate pizza, her son said he liked it a lot, she also had her part, but less than his son. She drank little alcohol, the occasional beer and wine with meals. She enjoyed martinis (she did not say how much she drank). An appointment was scheduled for a month later, to see the evolution of her diet.

******

PA-00.

Patient: an elderly lady. Diagnosis: Diabetic retinopathy (right eye affected). The lady was diagnosed with diabetes, but at a very advanced stage.

Key concepts about diabetic retinopathy discussed in this consultation: - Why diabetic retinopathy is important. Diabetic retinopathy develops over time, but may not cause symptoms until it is very advanced (the case in point).

Diabetic retinopathy can damage eyesight and remains a very significant cause of blindness in the working population.

DT: You have to take care of your diabetes, to reduce the risk of developing diabetic retinopathy in the other eye and to slow down the rate at which it occurs. We can't allow it to end up affecting the other eye. You know that would mean a high risk.

The signs and symptoms of diabetic retinopathy were explained as follows:

The earliest changes are called rebound retinopathy. Small changes develop in the blood vessels that look like small red dots. These are called microaneurysms.

Larger red dots are called retinal haemorrhages. They are found inside the retina and are like a bruise on the skin. Rebound retinopathy does not affect vision and does not need treatment.

Over time, the blood vessels can narrow and the retina can become starved of oxygen and nutrition. Different signs can be seen in the retina at different stages along this progression. This is called pre-proliferative retinopathy.

The woman had already been referred to the hospital for further tests during the last few weeks, where signs of the disease had been detected (in the eye).

The doctor said that the stage of the disease would be examined to see if laser treatment could be used to reduce the risk of sight loss. This technique was used in this hospital, but some tests had to be carried out, because it was always applied in the initial stages, not all patients were suitable for its implementation.

The appearance of retinopathy is directly related to the time of evolution of the disease and metabolic control. These alterations in the retinal microcirculation cause two physiopathological phenomena: capillary closure with the resulting ischaemia or extravasation of intravascular content to the stroma causing edema.

DT addresses the other relevant aspect of seeing diabetic retinopathy as a marker of the diabetic patient's health status. The presence of proliferative diabetic retinopathy signals that the patient is at increased cardiovascular risk.

The ophthalmologist was going to review the patient, as a classification of the severity of the DR was essential, valid both for him and for the other doctors who could treat the diabetic retinopathy of the PA.

For the time being, DT showed him some pictures of eyes, as an orientation and theoretical explanation. In one of the photos, retinal haemorrhages appeared in less than 20 in all four quadrants (according to his words). In the other photo, the alterations were severe intraretinal haemorrhages of more than 20 in each of the four quadrants (more severe).

She would now undergo some tests. When she had finished she could leave, she would be called back for a check-up, analysis of the results and, subsequently, a decision on the treatment or steps to follow. The woman seemed serene and calm. She was accompanied by an older son.

PA-09.

This is one of those cases that proves the doctors are right when they argue that most patients lie when being asked about their medical history and/or medications. It was a man who was scheduled to undergo "galstones" surgery. He gave the impression of lying a lot, as he had many surgeries performed in his home country but did not mention it.

The DT had his patient file, submitted presumably by the primary care physician and, from what I could understand, he was verifying the data face to face with the patient. We must not forget that this is a pre-surgery procedure, that is to saying, the patient's details are contrasted, and then, he will have to come back another day with a previous appointment (as it is logical) to undergo the surgery.

Well, the DT begun with his questions, mainly related to previous surgeries performed by the patient. The patient said in theory that his only problem was the "galstones" that he was going to have surgery on, but after the DT insisted.

The PA-09 admitted that he had had another surgery in his country of birth, which although I did not have a good understanding of why, had a connection with the one that was going to be carried out, in principle because of the area affected, which was very close to the one that would now have to be intervened on.

It should not be forgotten that in most cases, these sessions are organized just for that, that is to say, so that the surgeon can be sure that there are no extra risks before the surgery.

The DT kept on with his questions and, now after being pushed again, the patient admitted that he had also been in the surgery room in his country due to a knee injury, an accident that he could not describe, but the surgery did occur.

PA-09: that was just a minor intervention. I don't even remember anymore.

The DT asked PA-09 to take off the top of his clothes and to please sit on the stretcher next to us. PA did so willingly. The DT had pulled the curtain and could hear and translate properly, but I could not now see PA-09 without part of his clothes.

After a quick check, the DT asked the PA-09 what were some marks he had (I don't know exactly where), he spoke again hesitantly, but finally admitted that they were marks from another surgery he had also undergone in his country, he said that he had forgotten to have it done, now he remembered.

Although I could not see PA-09 and the location of his marks, I could sense from the DT's comments that he did not like the scenario, not knowing about the surgical procedure, because it was very close to the area that was going to be intervened. The PA-09 responded with quick quotes, he was starting to get restless. The PA wanted at all costs to go through surgery as soon as possible.

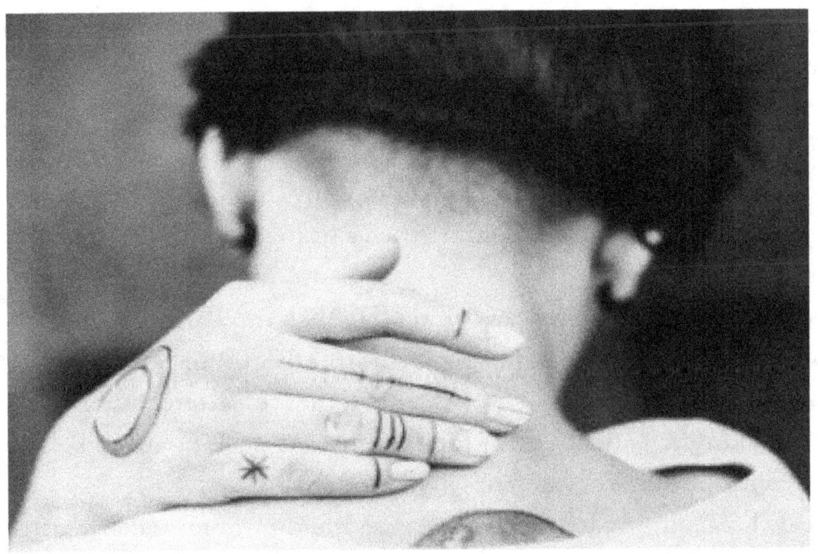

He was asking how much recovery time he was going to need. He was concerned about being available at once, as he didn't want to lose his boss's trust by missing too much time from work. The DT kept checking the recent history, including blood tests and so on, listened to the patient's words, but did not react at the moment.

In my estimation, she was carefully reviewing all the data to make sure that these unknown surgeries would not affect the pending process with the galstones.

Finally, he raised his head and responded to PA-09 regarding the recovery time. PA-09 was unhappy that it was too long and said that he could not wait that long, that something would have to be done.

By now PA-09 was dressed again and the curtain had been drawn so my task was back to where it started, the three of us sitting around the table.

Now came the medication checks that he was taking, there was a good assortment of pills. However, there were a couple of them, which appeared in the report and, at first, the PA-09 did not mention, then he reacted to the DT's persistent insistence and said that it was true that he was taking what he said he was taking, that he had forgotten to explain it the first time.

In these cases, there is an extra effort for the IT, I mean that the PA-09 answers, but the DT keeps pushing the question (he asks it twice) because he wants to catch the PA-09 in error (the DT has the family physician's records in front of him), then a strange scenario happens for the IT.

The question has to be repeated and more than translating (which you had already done) you have to demand the PA-09 to tell the truth, which can raise the anger of the PA, even if the critical circumstance has its origin in the patient's lie or forgetfulness (it is a bit hard to believe that someone forgets 3 surgeries in his body).

The DT called out for a few minutes, left the room and left us to ourselves. DT returned for a few minutes, made a call when he came back in and, after a brief silence, said that everything was in order and that the surgery date would be next week (we were on Friday).

He confirmed with the patient his availability for the proposed date and asked me to update the PA-09 on the dietary (food) details that he should follow before coming to the hospital on the day of the surgery. He was also asked if he was going to require IT before the procedure.

Treatment options for gallstones include (said the DT with a kind expression):

Surgery to remove the gallbladder (cholecystectomy). Surgical removal of the gallbladder may be recommended (this is the case here), as gallstones frequently recur.

Once the gallbladder is removed, bile flows directly from the liver to the small intestine, rather than being stored in the gallbladder. The gallbladder is not essential for life and its removal does not affect the ability to digest food, although it may cause diarrhea, which is often short-lived.

As PA-09 said good-bye, he thanked me for my assistance. I don't know if he had memory lapses or some other memory trouble remembering his medical records, but as a character, he was really a very kind and polite person.

He kept reiterating loudly that this long post-surgery time was not going to be acceptable, that he had to be at work in a few days, and that he was not going to allow it. There was some mutual laughter and I wished him a speedy recovery.

******

PA-62.

Partnered with his wife. He was in his 50s. In a wheelchair, due to the restricted mobility of his knee. He felt he could get around with crutches, but he used the wheelchair in the Hospital, with plenty of room in the corridors because it was more practical and faster to move around.

He had been involved in a motorcycle accident. His leg was trapped and the part that was broken was his knee. Several major injuries.

He had been at home for some time, now he returned to the hospital simply to schedule the appointment he had received, since he was going to be under surgery soon, it would be a few days of waiting.

He had damaged the internal ligament of his right leg.

DT: Although the length of the surgery can vary based on some factors (if you have meniscus reconstruction or a chondral problem), it is usual for a cruciate ligament surgery not to take much more than an hour.

DT: And, although it depends on everything running smoothly, the most usual is that you can go home the same day (if there are no complications and you have no associated pathologies).

They also told him things like:

-You are not a passive subject of the process. You have to participate with the surgical team at all times.

He and his wife were pleased to hear these and other preparatory tips which, although obvious, were still relevant:

- Stay active and practice strengthening exercises. The better your physical condition on the day of surgery, the easier your rehabilitation will be afterwards. Take care of your diet and try to keep your weight within healthy levels for your height and age.

- Seek family or external support for your hospital stay and for the first days of recovery after discharge.

- Prepare for your return home by removing possible obstacles in your home (carpets, cables, etc.) and try to find a high bed and a high, stable seat.

- If your house has several floors, try to install your bed on the lower one.

- Prepare the clothes and shoes you will take to the hospital. Wear comfortable clothes and closed-toed, non-heeled shoes. Do not forget a toiletry bag for personal hygiene and personal effects that you usually use such as glasses, hearing aids, dentures, etc. Do not carry valuables and remember to take your usual medication.

-You will not be able to eat anything between six and eight hours before the operation. You will not be able to drink any liquid in the two or three hours prior to surgery.

DT: It is quite normal to have limited knee mobility due to swelling and pain after surgery, and regaining that full knee movement (especially extension) can sometimes be exceedingly problematic. Therefore, regaining as much range of motion as possible before surgery is of utmost interest.

DT: Do not give up on physiotherapy until the last day, you will arrive at the surgery in the best condition: normal gait, no swelling, no pain, full mobility and a musculature in better shape, perfect to start the post-surgical rehabilitation in the best manner ever.

For a minute I was wondering if I were the patient, I would also like to hear these kinds of suggestions. Sometimes the details can make a difference in the preparation or the progress of a surgical procedure, the details are really and truly crucial.

******

PA-72.

The appointments I had at this hospital were all very early, about 6.30 in the morning, to start at 7am. I remember the entrance to the hospital from the center of Middle, relatively straightforward with a huge straight driveway. The hospital is well communicated by public transport, the bus, being able to arrive from Middle and surroundings with a single transfer.

The area was always cold in the morning, very cold in the winter dawn. Few visitors at that time of day, so I accessed it by following the road from the center of town.

The traffic was always very heavy in this area. Good houses that looked austere and middle-class air to the area, to flow into the hospital located at the exit of the town I had to look for the place on my own, following the signs, on the second floor I could access without much fanfare after several detours usual when you go for the first time.

There was still no one there. The access door to the Ward was closed, there was a notice that the doorbell had to be rung. There were no chairs or anything else, I was standing on the side stairs waiting. In less than 10 minutes, some people arrived and looked inside without ringing for the meantime.

Before 7am a nurse opened the door and quizzed everyone about the purpose of the visit. Then she closed the door again. I acknowledged myself, there were about three more IT's from other languages.

The room was regaining its morning activity and it would be a matter of just waiting my turn to see which PA was mine. This was for pre-surgery on the same day. No data was entered on the chart, only the schedule. There was total privacy.

I had to wait in an adjoining room. The nurse needed time to figure out what my PA was. The room was cold, lonely, no one was there, only medical instruments and some stretchers on the side. There were no amenities. It was a little scary to be left alone.

I was being invited into the next room. Here there were multiple stretchers with PA's separated only by curtains, at the same exit. The nurse told me that the stretcher next to the window was my PA-72, that I should wait two minutes standing up, that the DT would come and explain to me what to do.

The DT arrived almost at once, told me that it would be simple, he would talk to her for the pre-surgery process that would take place the same morning, maybe in about two hours, as it is obvious that I would have to translate, the basic guidelines of the process would be outlined, exactly what the surgery was about and the risks.

I thought it was pretty much what I expected, I just didn't know that the procedure was on the same day, but I didn't think it mattered.

The DT said that a hysterectomy is an operation to remove a woman's uterus. The uterus is where the baby grows during pregnancy. A hysterectomy will stop her menstrual periods and she will not be able to get pregnant again. In her case, due to the severity and, other issues already mentioned, the fallopian tubes are also removed.

We went inside the curtains, the PA-72 was on the bed, standing a young man of about 20 years old, who introduced himself as her son. The first formalities of the questionnaire would be done by a nurse, and then the DT would be present, but without intervening.

The son would also be present but without participating. By the way, the woman was fully awake and spoke clearly. There were no communication breakdowns.

The PA-72 was extremely motivated, she explained to me sideways with her son's gaze, that they had been expecting the operation for a long time, that she had been in a lot of pain and that this surgery was a miracle for her. She also told me that I was a good person and that she thanked me for my help. She made some religious references giving thanks and praying with her head held high.

There was a lot of noise in the background, I could hear another IT in the next curtain explaining and translating, I think it was in Polish. I could see that there would be several surgeries and the doctors were starting their activity with energy and performance at this time of the morning.

I approached a little closer to PA-72, and she took the opportunity to hold my hand, something that made me feel a tad uncomfortable. The son noticed, looked at me and said nothing. As soon as I could, I withdrew my hand. I felt a certain headache, very mild, maybe I woke up too early.

The nurse was showing me the form and reading it. It was a mandatory requirement to be explained to the PA prior to the procedure. I would have to sign the form and the final part of the risk consent form. The PA-72 signed without hesitation.

It had been underlined that hysterectomy is known to be a safe and quick recovery procedure, although it may present some possible complications, such as bleeding, wound infection, or injury to neighboring organs, among others.

The DT described more details about the intervention. It would be carried out through one of the usual access routes in gynecology. I am talking about abdominal hysterectomy with access through the abdomen. It would be an open surgery, involving a wide incision of the entire abdominal wall transversely above the pubis. It was applied in this case because of the extreme severity.

The patient presented uterine bleeding and constant pelvic pain for a long time, with no reaction to pharmacological treatment. It was not surprising that she was happy to see the day of the surgery come and get rid of that pain (as she herself admitted).

It was less than an hour, maybe shorter, the DT had made a detailed but quick explanation of everything. There was no time to lose, there were many patients in other beds who were also going to be intervened the same morning.

I tried to leave calmly, I had nothing more to do, everything had been fully covered and validated by the PA-72, she knew exactly what she had to do and what was the process.

4. Collecting Bloodied Polyps

PA-28.

PA-28 said that he was a newcomer to *Middle*, working in a restaurant as a cook, and he was bleeding in his stool. The doctor had recommended an endoscopy to be sure that it was nothing dangerous. This patient had two polyps removed, as I will be detailing.

If there are several polyps, the patient is advised to come back another day, and proceed with the others (to avoid the risk of bleeding). In any case, I have had several patients and none of them were in this dilemma (to come back another day).

Oddly enough, in the hospital where I did my work, they required that the patient be assisted during the whole process (before, during and at the end), or in other words, it was necessary to be physically present when the procedure was being performed, in case something needed to be explained to the PA-28.

We were in the waiting room, PA-28 asked me what the brochure he had just picked up on the table said about his procedure, and I translated it for him:

We were in the waiting room, PA-28 enquired what the brochure he had just picked up on the table had to do with his procedure, and I translated it for him:

Endoscopy is a non-surgical procedure used to examine a person's digestive tract. Using an endoscope, a flexible tube with a light and camera attached, the physician can view images of the digestive tract on a color television monitor.

During an upper endoscopy, the endoscope is easily inserted through the mouth and throat into the esophagus, allowing the physician to view the esophagus, stomach and upper small intestine.

Similarly, endoscopes can be inserted into the large intestine (colon) through the rectum to examine this area of the intestine. This procedure is called a colonoscopy, depending on how far into the colon the colon is examined (this would be the test that PA-28 would pass).

PA-28 thought was well explained, better than what the nurse said the other day. Since there was time to wait and as he was showing interest, I translated more of the booklet for him:

Doctors usually suggest an endoscopy to evaluate:

- Stomach pain.
- Ulcers, gastritis or difficulty swallowing.
- Bleeding from the gastrointestinal tract.
- Changes in bowel habits (chronic constipation or diarrhea).
- Polyps or growths in the colon.

The doctor may utilize an endoscope to take a biopsy (removal of tissue) to detect the presence of disease. Endoscopy may also be used to treat a digestive tract disorder.

For example, not only can the endoscope detect active bleeding from an ulcer, but devices can be passed through the endoscope that can stop the bleeding. In the colon, polyps can be removed through the endoscope to prevent the development of colon cancer.

For the time being, I felt that this was sufficient translation. The information read perfectly reflected the test he would pass.

PA-28 spoke to me about his past life without prompting. He mentioned his trip to a country in South America and how, after finding a young woman, he had married and finally stayed 15 years in that country (which was not his country of origin). Now, he had come to Middle because he had been offered a job in a restaurant as a chef.

He told me very briefly about the area of Middle where the restaurant was located and also shared with me details of the cuisine that was served there (I hadn't really asked any questions).

This was quite usual, because from the moment the patient arrived there was always a waiting time for the acknowledgement of forms giving time for conversation, which was not always easy.

I mentioned that the nurse had told us to wait in this room until further notice. He told me that his restaurant was good, that it had expensive dishes but that there were good customers and that everything was going well, although his salary was not very high either. He also said that he was working very hard and that perhaps this stress had led him to some extent to have this upset stomach for which he was now in the clinic.

For my part, I simply nodded my head, barely spoke, the truth is that although I always tried to avoid familiarizing myself with the PA in these cases, there was little I could do because he was taking the initiative and I was supposed to accompany him while he was in the waiting room.

The nurse signaled me that we could go to the next room. There he would take the laxative, put on the gown and would have to answer several questions to fill out the form. So we did, first were the questions and statements, where, as usual, he was asked about medication, if he was taking it, various aspects of this stuff, and then he was made aware of the risks that existed when doing this procedure.

Afterwards, he was made aware of the risks involved in having this type of examination. Typically, this part was indicated calmly and repeatedly, waiting for the interpreter to make all the guidelines very clear.

The PA-28 would have to confirm that he had understood and finally had to sign the entire form. In this case, I also had to sign in a mandatory way, in that very subtle box where it said interpreter.

Once done, we were taken to another room where we were no longer alone, there were other patients waiting for our turn, all in gowns and ready for the procedure.

This is where you change clothes and take the laxative. It is taken to help clean the area to be checked. As you would expect, it takes about 30 minutes to take the laxative before it takes effect. During this time I must be at the PA's side.

While PA-28 was in the restroom, I sat in a very cozy armchair next to another patient. He seemed lonely and began to talk to me as if he had known me for a long time, telling me his nationality, name and what he had done before coming to the hospital, if he had been to Middle I don't knew why for personal reasons.

I nodded and, thankfully, PA-28 came back, talking to other patients in this setting is not always reassuring.

I was asked if he was feeling alright and he said everything was fine, he just didn't know the appointment was taking so long. He was now wearing a long blue gown. I don't really know why they gave it to her in blue, but it was what was around.

He asked me what to do now. I told him that he should just wait until the laxative took effect and then follow the procedure that he could already imagine.

He fixed his eyes on me and told me that, yes, of course, everything was in order and that he would do whatever was needful. I reminded him that I was only the IT, and that everything he said was a translation of what the nurse had said, and that if he preferred we could call her back at any time, that's what we were there for. PA nodded and sat down in the next chair.

As for me, I was spending my time browsing through some magazines. There were a lot of sports, travel, political and other magazines. A lot of assorted magazines. PA-28 started talking about his life again (without my asking him anything). He said that he was 58 years old, that he was at an age when illnesses started to come, and that one had to be prepared.

His wife, he said, had stayed in the country where he had been living for the last few years, with their only daughter of about 15. But if everything went well, she would visit him very soon, they were preparing to travel very soon, and that this made him very excited because he had missed her and his daughter very much since he had moved away.

He was telling me that he missed going out dancing with her on Saturdays, and that he couldn't forget his daughter, which was the hardest thing about being in the new country, because he liked his job and the salary was decent.

He went on to say that he now was living in Middle (not far from this hospital) and that he shared a flat with another man who also worked in the same restaurant and who was of the same nationality as his wife, although they were not related to each other.

He told me that the cohabitation since his arrival in Middle was smooth, his flatmate was a friend and they understood each other well, but of course, after several years living with his wife and daughter, the change had been abrupt, because everything was completely reversed.

He droned on with his story, for my part, I just nodded and looked at the tennis pictures in one of the magazines, I think they were from the Middle Tennis tournament that same year.

At this point, given that we had not yet been called, and that he was still going on with his family story, I decided to engage him in a bit of chitchat. I told him that some time ago I had also travelled a bit in South America and that I coincidentally knew something of the city where he had lived. He seemed to be pleased with my words.

The patient next to us had already been called, which made me think that slowly but surely everything was on course and we would be next. I had experience and knew for myself that sometimes it could take up to 2.30 or even 3 hours depending on various circumstances.

He told me that he was very fond of meat, he meant red meat, which was prepared in differing manners. The roasts, the baked, roast varieties where he could understand he was quite good at preparing it, hence, his job. But now what he was trying to tell me was that he also liked to eat that particular type of food.

As I could understand from his slower way of speaking, it was as if he was leaving in the air the doubt of whether this prolonged intake of food could be affecting the health of his intestine, or at least that was the idea I could visualise, given that it is well known that there have been several studies for years on this type of food situation, some studies as usual are against its excessive consumption and others support its consumption in the opposite way.

It was as if by making the comment, he gave me time to give my answer, as if he was indirectly asking me what I thought about it. I replied that I was not there to make dietary assessments, that I was only the interpreter, but that if he wanted to know, from time to time I had a beef steak with potatoes and that I liked it, and that for the moment my intestine was fine.

He had a soft smile, and said: "Yes, yes, yes, of course, a good steak always goes well with a good wine.

He began to inquire if I had ever had any such health problems. I told him that for the moment I had not yet, but that these things are quite common nowadays. In fact, if you read any article or magazine on these issues, you can see how common these diseases are not only in Middle, but also in other countries.

The awareness of these issues is increasing from a social point of view. Stress, pace of life, mobility, eating habits, all of these were affecting our health. I tried to shift the conversation.

He told me that I was beginning to feel a tingling in my stomach, the laxative was working. I had to continue the process. He got up and went back to the bathroom. I was able to continue with the tennis magazine, waiting for everything to go forward.

After a short time, the PA-28 reappeared, everything was fine. The nurse told us that we could now go to the exam room, where the test was to be carried out. I was relieved. We got up and went to the ward, which was far away in a separate corridor.

To avoid patients getting lost and not having to waste time escorting them, they had devised an easy system, there was a blue line on the ground, we had to follow the line and it would take us to the X-ray room. The PA-28 was now very quiet and without saying a word, he let me guide him.

We arrived in the room, a doctor was at the door, I introduced myself as the IT, he told me what my positioning and placement should be roughly during the process and, he told the PA-28 to go to the stretcher, which was naturally where the operation would take place. There were more staff in the room, two women, and another doctor, a total of 4 people in addition to us.

The room resembled a real life X-ray room, lots of devices, several PC screens or similar, an X-ray table surrounded by all kinds of instruments that were unfamiliar to me, and a very large annex where the nurses and the doctor were preparing their utensils and notes. One of the screens was in the PA-28's alignment, i.e. positioned so that he could also see the intervention if he would like to.

I was told in outline what I was to translate for him and he was asked to lie down on the stretcher. I placed myself in the indicated position, so as not to get in the way of the process. PA-28 was very calmed, he listened to my words and nodded his head.

Everything was proceeding very well, there was enough space and everyone present seemed to know what they had to do. All very professional.

The process commenced. Two polyps were removed. Everything was running smoothly. Nothing out of the norm they said, so that PA-28 would be at ease. Additional comments were made. PA-28 was calm with no disturbances.

At the end of the proceedings, it was necessary to finalize the process in another room. Another nurse explained how they were managing and completed the screening of his case, another exit document had to be signed (in this case I didn't have to sign) and the last guidelines were given, which dates I would receive the result and some additional questions.

The PA-28 was very serene and simply listened to my translation and nodded his head. At no time had he complained, no pain or anything like that, I was relieved that everything was going so swimmingly.

He was instructed that the removal of the two polyps did not mean that he had anything serious. The polyps were simply being extracted as a precaution and to study whether they were benign or not.

Now it was necessary to wait for the results, but this explanation was always made (in other cases I had also done the same), and it was made because when told that polyps were being excised, some patients associated that this was a sign of something serious and, of course, the professional's obligation was to be clear about this.

In most incidents, the polyps caused the bleeding (which, let's not forget, was the reason for this action), but nothing more, when they were removed they stopped bleeding. PA-28 grasped the idea perfectly well and nodded with relief and gratitude for the help. He had a carefree air about him.

We said our goodbyes and went our separate ways, trying to be discreet to avoid further intimacy with PA-28 and to avoid further chatter. PA-28 dropped a card in my hand with the address of his restaurant wordlessly, I put it in my pocket, turned around and went in the direction of the underground exit.

******

PA-26.

PA-26 had been working in *Middle* for two years since she had arrived from his home country. She had been bleeding when she defecated, the doctor had recommended endoscopy. PA-26 was the first woman I had ever had to perform one of these sessions.

She joined me in the ante-room as usual, but she hardly said a word, she seemed quite reserved, or just preferred not to say anything. I felt very comfy, a distance is always better, no familiar words.

We went to the next room. I was explaining to the nurse the antecedents (they were duplicates, but according to the DT they were all needed to complete her file):

- Bright red or very dark blood in the stool.
- Abdominal discomfort, frequent gas pains, bloating, fullness and cramps.
- Constant tiredness or fatigue.

The DT noted, she was very serious. She carried on with the usual form of questions, and the final signature confirming that everything had been understood. However, PA-26 wanted to add a few details.

DT: It is important to recall that the symptoms and signs of colorectal cancer listed in this section are the same as those of highly common non-cancer conditions such as haemorrhoids and irritable bowel syndrome (IBS). When cancer is suspected, these symptoms are more likely to have started recently, to be severe and long-lasting, and to change over time.

DT: By being alert to symptoms or signs of colorectal cancer, it may be possible to detect the disease at an early stage, when it is more likely to be treated successfully. However, many people with colorectal cancer do not have any symptoms or signs until the disease is advanced, so they should be screened regularly. Hence the importance of this test. Remember, you should never think you have cancer because you don't until there is full confirmation.

I think he made these disclosures because he saw PA-26 looking quite tense and worried. PA-26 listened, but showed no signs of relief, just kept stern.

We went to the operating room. I noticed from the start that she was not in a comfortable position. She paced around several times before accepting the invite to lie down on the gurney. She remained in the position indicated for the IT. PA-26, she was shaking her head and asking why there were so many monitors. She said she thought the camera insertion would be through the mouth.

I brought this to the attention of the DT. It was made clear to her, that it had been previously been explained to her. Her test was anal intercourse. She was asked to please get into the right position. As she looked uneasy, I did a repetition of what had been said while the DT looked at me. She was asked not to move. The PA was really uneasy.

I think she had a slightly altered picture in her head of what the process would be like. I could tell from her reacting that she was not at ease. The DT, who was aware of everything, made some comments to relax her, things that had nothing to do with the intervention, but she didn't react.

She was still looking very grave, and turned her head towards me two or three times. On the orders of the DT, I told her to turn all the way round and not to move, to look at the monitor on her left so that she could follow what was being done to her and, please, not to move. Just relax, the process would be over soon.

There were no polyps to remove. She was advised to follow up the bleeding (if there was any more) with her doctor. The outcome was very positive.

We went to the discharge room. She kept a very straight face. They reminded her again to follow up but made it clear that there were no polyps. The nurse asked her several times if she was ok. PA-26 said she wanted to cover the form to leave because she was hungry. As usual I helped her cover and translate the final questions.

She left in a rude manner, there was no farewell. I saw that she was taking the wrong exit direction, I let her know and I turned the wrong way to avoid contact. The truth is, I don't know exactly what was wrong with her, because the result had been so successful.

It was apparent that she felt awkward during the session, it was very evident that she was not able to relax, but it showed that she was not able to open up and express what the trouble was, unless it was just a temporary nervousness. One of the DT's also had these perceptions and, he let me know. He told me, during the final rinse, to try to find out what his state of mind was.

I was not in a positive frame of mind either. I tried to talk to the DT for a few minutes, remembering the APS's insights regarding the discussion of the emotive input. Following engagement with the patient, the psychologist should be aware that the interpreter may have found areas of the engagement conflicting or distressing:

- While a brief discussion or debriefing is likely to follow the session, the psychologist should be aware of his or her ethical responsibility for the interpreter's psychological well-being and the degree of support he or she wishes to provide in these circumstances.

- The psychologist may provide the interpreter with some contact details of support services if they feel that the interpreter is at risk of distress and will need help. If the interpreter has experienced any distress, it is important for the psychologist to be aware that this may also affect the accuracy of the interpretation of the client's consultation. She was one of the few patients that I was able to meet in the street by chance, I mean one day by chance. It was a chance meeting near my home, I had just come out of a supermarket and I noticed that this woman was facing me on the same pavement. I remembered her face, it had only been a few days since the medical visit.

PA-26 avoided the greeting, lowered her head and didn't want to hear from me. I hesitated, but it was too blatant that she didn't want to say "hi". Maybe she thought my help was not quite right or maybe she was disappointed with the medical care, hard to say.

In truth, my idea was to say hello and ask her how she was, if she had recovered, or just to say goodbye, but things are sometimes like that, there is no reason to explain. I would have liked to know what was going through her mind.

*****

PA-47.

When I introduced myself he was surprised and said:
You are not black! And he laughed and said: " You're not black!. And he started laughing. I laughed too, making light of the comment.
I told him: there might not be any black IT staff members available, and smiled again. He nodded, with a very pleasant gesture, and held out his hand.
It was for it was for another endoscopy. The process starts, as one would expect, with the paperwork and forms, and then moves on to warnings, explaining certain risks of the procedure that the patient must accept (the IT's work is very critical at this point), then on to the ingestion of the laxative. I estimate a wait of about 40 minutes depending on the number of PA's in the room.
Being a bit of a gossip, I would say, that this phase is almost amusing, you can share a waiting room with several patients before they come in, dressed in housecoats, slippers and unfriendly faces, little less than a Vaudeville play. Each one endures the wait as best he or she can, a

magazine here and there, or various conversations, depending on the mood of each one.

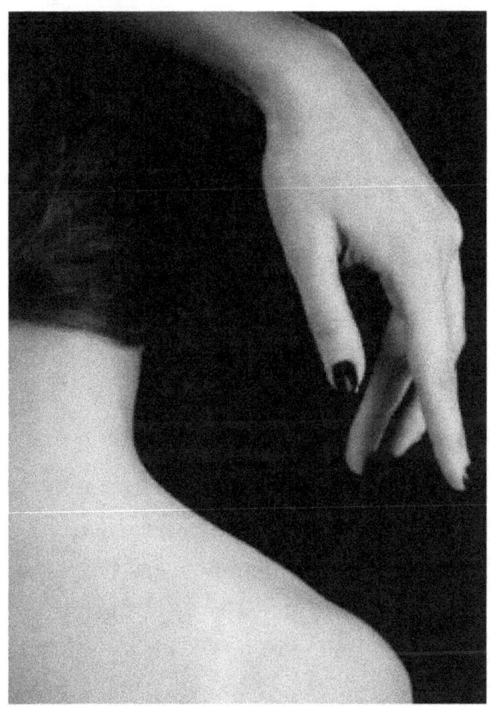

Now comes the medical feedback, the nurse asking questions about the medical history, although it has been done before, now with the presence of the IT it is intended to establish the patient's background, diseases, potential past surgeries, medication, to get to the key point, the risks of the endoscopy.

In essence, there is nothing special about this, anyone who has been to the dentist to have a tooth removed will remember that he have to sign off on the risks of the extraction. It is the same here. By the way, this form must also be signed by the IT.

There were some enlightenments from PA-47, but they did not touch the process. He was a man with a long medical history. The nurse repeated to him to please always tell the truth because if he omitted any health issues or surgeries performed that were not indicated in the history, this could impact on the process to be performed and increase the risk of unwanted secondary situations. The PA-47 smiled, and nodded.

He asked if he had to follow a diet or something like that after the process, if the nutritional issue was important. The nurse said that it was not primary, but that as a recommendation he could follow the following (2-3 days):

DT: After a colonoscopy, it is advisable to follow a soft and light diet to facilitate the recovery of the intestinal tract. For example chicken broth, white rice, mashed potatoes, yoghurt. It is important to avoid heavy, spicy and fibrous foods until the digestive tract has fully recovered.

The intestinal tract may be weakened and the intestinal flora may be affected due to the cleansing required before the procedure. It is important to restore the intestinal flora for optimal recovery.

DT: It is recommended that you gradually increase the amount and choice of foods in your diet over the next few days, observing how your body reacts. If you experience abdominal pain, nausea, vomiting or other symptoms, consult your GP before continuing your normal diet. But in principle, there is no need to worry because there are likely to be no side effects.

PA-47 I listened to the arguments put forward without further comment. Of all the cases I had attended, I was the first to ask about these dietary issues, which were usually commented on by the nurse only in passing.

His face was very punished, perhaps because of the sun. It reminded me of some people who worked at sea, sailors who, after many years of work, had the skin of their faces very punished by the sun and the sea salt. Their eyes were fixed on me, waiting for the translation. He did not understand a word of English.

Everything went well. Two polyps were removed. His attitude was excellent, with hardly any questions. He was always helpful and facilitated the work of the DT's. My assistance was hardly needed. He was clear about what was going to be done, you could almost say he was familiar with the process.

Final room: He asked again about food. He said something he had not mentioned before, that he had been vomiting for the last few days. The nurse made some final remarks:

DT: Do not drink stimulants such as alcohol, beer, tobacco or coffee. Because these irritants will irritate the stomach lining, causing stomach damage.

He was informed that the removed polyps would now be sent to the specialist department to find out if they were benign. He learned the result in a few days. For the time being he was to follow the advice of the DT and to let him know if his bleeding continued or if there were any changes. PA-47 listened without saying anything.

When we said goodbye he again made a comment about the fact that he had been assigned a non-black IT. It seems to me that he had a sense of humour and that he was a very nice chap. I hope that the comments were really ironic and that he was not worried about such a trivial matter as skin colour, when the most important thing was to know that he did not have cancer.

5. After-Meal Unwanted Touching

PA-101.

This one particular case, which I will refer to as PA-101, involved an alleged sexual assault on a girl who was a student at a High School. Among those attending the meeting were her family (she was not present), a sister, her father and mother, a supervisor, a coordinator, two teachers from the high school, a psychologist from the high school, a therapist from out of the high school, and the IT.

There was no one from the police or direct governmental bodies, nor was there anyone directly related to the alleged aggressor. The accused young man was an Englishman, they both studied at the same school.

These meetings are held in an attempt to seek agreement and avoid a court case. The function of the IT, as is obvious, is to break down and help with the language barrier of the family of the alleged assaulted, who did not speak English fluently.

Cases of alleged attempted rape are really complex from the interpreter's professional point of view. The meetings are set up as a background review of the case being investigated, assistance to the alleged victim and, on multiple occasions, no prior facts are provided to the IT, making their task more arduous, in addition, the family of the victim does not always attend with a degree of knowledge of the scope of the meetings.

As these are informal meetings, I was notified that they had already had another one a few weeks before, which the girl's father had not been able to attend, so this day they would try to determine key issues in the presence of all the family involved.

The meeting had already had another IT (previous session), so my task was to catch up as quickly as possible to be ready to translate the events, opinions and so on (this point represents another difficulty for the IT, since in my opinion it is much easier when it is the same IT who attends the different meetings of the same case).

Having set the background, let's move on to the meeting's activities. The coordinator exposes the case in a generic way. The assistants first tried to convince the family not to move forward with legal proceedings, perhaps other alternatives could be found.

The facts reported were based on the alleged attempted and completed rape that a young man had committed against the daughter of the family present at the meeting. No details were given today. This was basically the complaint that the family had filed with the police, which was supported by the young woman allegedly assaulted.

There was a police report, based on statements made by the young woman to the police, explaining the facts. The issue, according to the coordinator, was that it was not established whether the rape had been consummated. The young woman's testimony left doubts open for investigation, according to the police report.

The parents, really polite in their behavior, waited and listened to the experts present and, of course, to my translation. They did not interfere, they only listened, when their turn to speak came, they made it clear that they had full confidence in their daughter's deposition and that they were convinced that the rape had taken place and that they wished to proceed with the accusation.

The arguments were long and were really based on a range of opinions, of a psychological character, of behavior among teenagers, of sexuality in the couple at that age, of presumed doubts about the testimony, of evaluation of the circumstances of the events, of the time that the young woman had been in the High School, the intricacy was remarkable and the duration of the meeting was getting to be long.

The truth is that almost 100% of those present were trying with their opinions to convince the family that it might not be the most suitable option to keep on with the charges.

This is how the father understood it, and after more than two hours of meeting he was starting to get a little nervous and expressed his disapproval (always in a very polite tone, of course).

The truth is that I myself was about to suggest a break (although I would not do it). The coordinator, however, recognized the heaviness of the meeting and proposed a 30-minute maximum presentation and final discussion as a way of closing the meeting.

The parties did not seem to be getting closer, the parents were even talking about leaving the country (almost certainly, they said) because their daughter was very emotional and they could not imagine living with her if she kept the sadness of the moment. The experts remained at their point of view, and they did not think it was very realistic for the lawsuit to go forward.

Little by little the time was running out and a final speech by the coordinator, with a screen included, put an end to this meeting of about 2.30 minutes, which turned out to be too long for the IT.

By chance, the coordinator questioned the family twice if they liked the translation she was doing, which made me a bit surprised, because they had not ever complained about it and it was not the norm. They agreed that everything was fine with them.

Let's look at the indications contained in the BPS regarding the *Pre-consultation meeting:*

The interpreter will be in a better position to interpret accurately if he or she clearly understands the purpose of the meeting and the role of all parties involved.

The psychologist can schedule a pre-consultation meeting with the interpreter prior to the first session to inform the interpreter of the purpose of the consultation (e.g., obtain information about the client's developmental history, assess mental health status) and provide an overview of the session (e.g., a description of the activities that will take place, such as interviews, discussions, and questions).

This allows the interpreter to ask questions and clarify terminology. This conversation can take place over the telephone. If the psychologist intends to use a psychometric assessment during the consultation with the client, this should be discussed with the interpreter during the pre-consultation meeting.

If appropriate, the psychologist can inform the interpreter that the content is likely to be distressing, particularly if the psychologist anticipates that distressing events such as conflict, violence, suicide, self-harm or family crisis will be discussed. The interpreter may be better prepared to manage the traumatic nature of a meeting if he or she is warned that he or she may find it disturbing.

This is really both intriguing and worrisome. Because placing the IT close to the family leads to the family members trying to liaise with the IT. Especially by placing me next to the father (who had not attended the previous meeting). Something absolutely not recommended.

The parent will obviously look for ongoing support from the IT, and will generate interference. If the IT is placed in a neutral point, things change, and the work can be carried out with a minimum of professionalism. The placement next to the father was totally mistaken.

There are other factors, such as the tension of the meeting itself, there is almost always a state of pre-tension, which, as is to be expected, comes from the side of the family, many times they have been misinformed about what is expected of them in this meeting and, other times they do not even know exactly why they are there. The IT is also not briefed. The difficulties are really self-evident.

Regrettably, none of this was taken into any consideration today, even though I tried to clarify these issues at the beginning, but there are days when the hosts would rather look the other side or simply have no idea how to carry out their duties.

******

PA-102.

It was a very doubtful case according to the initial evidence and, the rapporteurs' outlook. The girl had bruises, but the police did not guarantee that they could not be self-inflicted, that was an initial characterization in the eyes of the mother, unresolved stuff to figure out and that is what was pending. The whole process was open and in pre-investigation.

Meeting attendees: Mother of the assaulted. One sister. Two psychologists. A teacher. An organizer. A supervisor. Another participant (not presented). The IT.

On the one hand, it was given pieces of news about the support and the aid that the assaulted woman had been already receiving. On the other side, allegations were made on the part of the accused, doubting the credibility of the explanations given by the alleged victim. There were no medical reports.

On this opportunity, I requested in advance that I should be placed in a neutral position (this was granted). I was closer to the mother than to the other attendants, but the position was quite accurate.

The sister had the appearance of being about 18 years old and was next to the mother of the other side. I do not know the age of the alleged victim, although keeping in mind that she was in high school, I estimate that she was in the 15-18 age range. I say she was in high school because there was a teacher and a psychologist from the high school, I had not been offered any prior info.

On the opposite side of the table, all the attendees except for the organizer who was at the head of the table, with the screen in the background.

The victim had received psychological help, although she had stopped attending classes in the last few weeks. This aspect was discussed and the mother had been asked about her opinion, the state of the victim and the choice not to attend classes.

The mother had informed the school about the withdrawal for the time being, although she had only done so by phone call, hence the further explanations that were now being solicited.

The psychologist of the school made his assessment, once it was judged to be a mental health choice rather than a potential physical injury. According to his assessment, the physical status of the assaulted was positive.

The teacher also made his assessment, which spoke of the negative aspects of a long absence and that he expected an effort on her part to attend classes as soon as possible, and also stated that the intellectual activity at the school and the interaction with her classmates would always be beneficial, much more so than being locked up at home.

The hostess offered some brief remarks to the mother, telling her some relevant news about what had been done for them so far and that they had been treated psychologically, but that the young woman had not wanted to cooperate, which is why they now needed to clarify all this at this meeting in order to reach a mutual understanding in the future. She was also reminded that the lack of the father (for work reasons) was not good news, the father should be involved in these sessions. There was a reply from the mother who thought it was beneficial to protect the girl and not to force her to go to classes for the moment, as for the husband, she said that she would try to convince him for a next meeting (if there was one), she said that he was quite frustrated and preferred to avoid strained scenes.

The coordinator reminded him that these meetings were for them, i.e. the affected family, and were aimed at their own private support.

The mother was a bit on edge and said that she did not understand why the police report had not been handled. The coordinator reminded her that an investigation process was underway, although the idea of this meeting was not to focus on the complaint itself.

The other daughter, sitting next to the mother, said nothing, just listened, I think she must have understood a lot of English, because she hardly looked at me when I was translating for her mother.

The meeting became more and more tensioned, they remembered the details of the so-called aggression, the way in which the events had occurred and the date. The mother became more nervous, the truth is that the assistants, I don't know if consciously or unconsciously, acted as a block, as if putting pressure on her and, of course, she had no one to defend her.

The supervisor, who was sitting on the side, said not one word, he was using his cell phone to type text messages (supposedly it was forbidden for all the attendees to access the room with their cell phones).

The coordinator returned to the charge, pointing out to the mother that although the trial was in process, they had been offering her the necessary support and that they regarded her posture as somewhat detached, she judged that the family should be more flexible, accept the counseling of those present, and handle the support offered in a new manner in the future.

New assessments of the facts were made, and the mother argued questions of ethics and family culture in defending her course of action. I tried to follow the translation in detail and to reflect her struggles, because it was possibly a culture shock that was hardly understood by some of the attendees.

This is a very common concern and in which the IT must put its greatest emphasis, not only by translating but also by mirroring the cultural ones, especially towards the affected person.

Be that as it may, the attendants' approach made this type of treatment problematic, it was very evident that they were trying to convince the mother to follow a path, which they would consider fitting for this circumstance, but which in principle was met with the family's rejection (let's not forget that it was a family from a South American country).

The coordinator looked at the screen behind her, but in reality it was turned off, it had not been used for the meeting. Another attendee gave new arguments. The mother seemed quite tired, it had been almost an hour and a half of meeting and, to tell the truth, no great progress could be detected.

She mentioned the duration of the meeting and, she said, she would offer another date with the same attendees, hoping that the father could also participate, in the meantime, as is logical, she asked her to inform the husband of what had been discussed today so that he would be aware of the status of the event.

The mother nodded, and one could guess a certain relief in her words as the meeting came to an end. The truth is that seeing the cases of no prior orientation and so many troubles in understanding other basic facts, I decided that in the future I would not attend any more meetings of this type if there was not a minimum of prior data.

I tried to make some brief culturally sensitive comments about the origins of the family involved to the supervisor, but he said that that was enough for today and that the meeting was not going to last, and that my job was only to translate and not to evaluate what was said.

I found this comment totally wrong, but I was not surprised either, because he had not said anything in the whole meeting and had only spent his mobile phone checking the internet's websites and his email.

I think someone should remind this supervisor of what is stated in the APS regarding *Cultural awareness*:

The provision of adequate interpretation and translation services is therefore crucial for cultural maintenance and for the realisation of a truly multicultural society.

An important consideration for psychologists working with a culturally diverse population is that language is only one component of effective service delivery. While the use of an interpreter in service delivery is essential, it alone is not sufficient for working with a multicultural clientele.

Mental health services need to develop culturally appropriate ways of supporting communities, which requires engagement with immigrants and refugees, provision of information about seeking help for mental health problems, and training of health professionals in communicating about these issues with diverse communities (e.g. cultural competence, safe cultural practice).

When, in addition to language, different cultural frameworks come into play, the likelihood of shared meaning developing is even more tenuous. In the interest of the clinical goal, the interpreter may intervene to ensure that both parties understand the messages being conveyed. In this sense, the interpreter can be said to function as a 'communication advocate'.

PA-41.

Case under study: custody separation of the children from their parents, three in total. One of them was less than a year old. The police had removed the children from the mother (who lived alone with them) a few days earlier. The social workers and psychologist explained the background to PA-41.

She was a very young girl, although it was stated that the children were all hers, she was not yet more than 25 years old by my reckoning.

Briefing: PA-41 was questioned about her personal backstory. At what time she had come to Middle, how she had two children with her at the time of her first trip (already from another European country than her own). Later, she had the third child, already in Middle.

A detailed review was made. She would disagree with some of the points, telling me to make it clear to them (me) that it wasn't like that, that she didn't agree with them. She was quite nervous.

It was not the first time that the social worker had dealt with her, as she had difficulties in supporting her family (children), and she had previously applied for social, psychological and financial help.

From what she said, she had not benefited much from them, she said that her financial problems had not improved. The DT reminded her that they had arranged decent housing for her and her children, implying that she had paid almost nothing (low rent).

Subsequently, her mother, who also resided in Middle, had been contributing a little financially and also taking care of the children when she had the time, as she did work, her mother that is.

The financial difficulties had increased with the arrival of another baby. There were three of them and she still didn't have a job that could support the family. This was now becoming a serious crisis, and the social assistance she was being offered was not enough, because the social worker was trying to keep her on her own.

The meeting had been one of constant tension from the beginning, although so far PA-41 had a sense of relative peace and quiet. Her mother was in the room, as was the only sister she had, who was a little younger than her.

Little by little, we moved on to the key point of the meeting. It had been less than a week since the police had come to her home and taken her children out of her care.

This was the reason for this meeting, to settle this matter, what had happened, what had been the reasons for the police to take this decision, how she was at the moment, and also what the guidelines would be in the future, because the children were not with her, and they would not come back to her so easily, there was a process to follow in these cases that lasted several months.

We had to get down to crunch time. The woman on trial was the mother herself, and there was no talk of physical violence, but rather of the mother's alleged carelessness in not feeding her children properly.

A neighbour had called the police because the PA's flat was noisy and was disturbing the neighbours. The police acted on the phone call and, when they reached the PA's home (according to the police report) she was drunk and surrounded by several friends (it was stated that there were four of them, all men, of the same nationality as her).

The police saw that her children were unattended and, seeing the mother in a drunken manner, entered the house to check if she at least had food for the children, they could see that the fridge was completely empty and that there was no food or items to make food anywhere.

In view of the alarming scenario, they immediately urged PA-41 to go and buy food for the children, while they (the police) would be at home waiting for her. The PA left the house signalling that she would go shopping at a local supermarket not too far away.

The real trouble, according to the police report, was that she took a very long time to return, allegedly two hours of waiting without any justification whatsoever.

They waited anyway. As soon as she returned home, and considering her lack of behaviour, it was interpreted by the police that she had done it on purpose to see if the police would be leaving.

In view of this attitude, and the fact that (police said) she was even having trouble expressing herself (understandably because of her drunkenness) they determined that they could not be given another chance.

The entire situation seemed untenable to them. She was having a party with several friends, totally drunk and without any food for her children (remember that one of them was less than a year old). The police then decided to take the children away for their own protection. When it came time to review what had occurred the night the police had removed her children, she became more nervous and could not suppress her tears. Although she listened to the whole story without pausing, she only looked at me. She just kept shaking her head at me, signalling her disagreement by shaking her head that it was not so, that she did not agree.

Those who were present inquired at this point whether he agreed with the facts. She said that it was true that there were friends at home, but that they were not having a party, that it was just a visit from acquaintances from her country who were working in Middle. She also pointed out that although they were having a few beers, she was not drunk.

On the question of going to the supermarket, she said that she did not know the area very well, that she had decided to get on a bus and had got on the wrong line, then when she realised she had to go back on another bus line and, without realising it, it had taken her a long time. PA-41 made it clear that she did not subscribe to the police version. She also added that she did not comprehend why the children were being taken and removed from her, particularly the youngest, the one who was less than a year old.

PA: I knew it was about control, I knew it was just going to be another tactic to cause as much chaos and pain in my life. And I just thought it was absolutely absurd. I was not having fun with many friends. I love my kids. I have an excellent relationship with them.

She went on to say that she was searching for employment, she thought she would soon be earning income support. In addition, her mother, who had been away on a trip to her country, had returned and would help her with childcare if she would start working.

Those present reminded her that she had a legal avenue to appeal the police report. But for the time being the process with her children would follow the usual route.

PA: I was basically shocked when I read the documents that were provided to me as to why this child was taken. I wish I'd never had the friends visit. You know, I wish I'd have just kept alone at home and not told anyone because now they're going to take my kids for so long time. They treat me as if I had beaten my children.

In this case she would be allowed to meet the children in a secure centre, on Saturdays, one saturday a month. To be switched to two saturdays a month, if everything runs as per the protocol.

PA-41. Saturday meeting with children.

I was able to be present a few days later at the first meeting with their children. It was in a centre in Middle, nicely set up, with the appearance of a primary school. PA-41 was able to enjoy the time with her children for more than two hours.

The DT on the premises allowed her to feed them and play with them, but she was harsh and forthright in her comments. At all times she was very demanding, in the sense of telling her the right thing to do. The PA displayed a positive approach and tried to keep the children as happy as she could. At times she seemed a bit lost.

PA-41 made a mistake, which the DT did not approve of. Although the room was well set up with several seats and tables, when it was time to feed the children, she simply used a kind of towel and put the food on top of it, on the floor. The DT corrected her straight away and asked her to always use a table to feed the children in the future.

The rest of the meeting was very low-key, some games and mother-son stuff. There was no insistence on the part of the DT with particular points.

At the next meeting, the PA was joined by her sister. She commented that she had found a job in a restaurant. She was excited about her new occupation. The DT was a little distrustful because, as she had said, before the children were taken away, the PA had worked three jobs in a short space of time and had left them very quickly, within a month or two.

The DT expressed her good luck and told her that if she would work and adapt well to her new circumstances, everything would be more comfortable, and the job would help her financial viability, which at the time was quite precarious.

I don't know how many meetings there were in the future or when she was able to recuperate custody (if that happened) because I never returned to these meetings.

*****

PA-42.

Domestic abuse case with withdrawal of custody of children. This meeting was only with the mother. In the following days another meeting would be held with the assistance of the husband.

She was a woman of about 45 years old. She was attending the meeting alone, there was a social worker and two other people (not introduced). There had been a succession of events over the last few months. The woman had reported violence from her partner. She had called the hotline several times, police patrols had been sent to her aid, often in the early hours of the morning.

So far, no drastic measures had been taken, the alleged aggressor always changed his attitude when he was confronted with the police. Now the scenario was changed.

We went to the relevant scene, that of the alleged assault. In this case, the PA-42 complains that her husband used a knife from the kitchen, she mentions a very large knife, and that he attempted to aggress her with this knife, although she was able to avoid it and hold on until the police came.

In essence what was being done today was to contrast her words, now in cold blood, with the police report generated on the night of the event. Due to the woman's temper that night, her degree of excitement, crying and screaming, and in view of the recurrence of the alleged actions, the police had taken the measure of removing the two children that the couple had in common, a boy and a girl, both minors.

As was only logical, this measure was taken because of the high level of injury they were at risk of receiving.

The woman was very serious, but relaxed, showing no signs of nervousness or similar for her children, in fact, one could say, she was relieved not to have to take care of her children. The professionals present informed her of other circumstances that she should be aware of, mainly from a legal point of view.

Let's not overlook the fact that these meetings are a warm-up, but there will be issues to discuss with the police or a legal team (her lawyer) in the future. What was certain, however, was that her children would be in guardianship. And from my past experience, that meant months or maybe years of waiting to get your children back.

As the meeting progressed and these kinds of issues were pressed, the woman seemed more and more upset. One could say that she was still absorbing the depth and reality of the matter.

She said that she and her children had a very good relationship, that she cared for them because they were her children, and that her only wish was to have them by her side.

She didn't understand why they withdrew from her, the father was to blame for the attitude with his violent actions, she didn't want to lose her children in any way, she loved them by her side. In addition, her concern for their food and basic issues was absolute, she was always looking out for them, she was searching for school options for them and that she loved them very much.

She was suffering domestic abuse, she said, but her children were on the sidelines, they were not the targets.

DT: All the of the evidence in this case has been considered by the family experts, on several occasions and in front of different psychologists. At all times we have acted in the best interests of the child. Throughout these proceedings, the child and you has been represented by an appointed guardian, independent of the local authority, to ensure that your views and wishes are heard.

The DT and those present took some notes, and repeated to her not to worry, that she would have the right to share moments with her children, despite the harshness of these circumstances, she would have her rights and would not stop seeing her children, let's say, that she should see it as a temporary, but necessary and beneficial step, as she would be totally protected in terms of her children's safety.

She was also made aware that her husband would in principle also have the right to have separate meetings to visit her children. After these successive meetings over a period of several months, a filter would be established, deciding which of the two would once again have custody of her children.

Their personal and professional status would also be assessed. For the time being, this was still too early, there were legal and derivative connotations, which would have to be followed up. On the other hand, it should not be ignored that they were both foreigners in Middle.

A complete background check was carried out, both had jobs, had sufficient means to support their families and were living on a rented basis. Several references were made in this environment, to corroborate the status of her husband from her own mouth.

Everything seemed pretty standard, the fact that they both had jobs, greatly improved their overall position, which seemed very stable from an economic point of view.

The assistants were gentle in their approach, I mean, they were very empathetic to the allegedly violent context, they facilitated the translation contact and made the meeting as easy as possible, so that the PA did not feel rejected. In fact, they did not emphasise much on the specific moment of the alleged aggression, the conversation had immediately moved on to the children's matter.

The children's plight and environment was the priority, rather than the alleged aggression. Nor was reference made (only in passing) to medical reports of assaults or physical marks, all of which, I presume, would be dealt with at another meeting, because today it was left aside, not followed up.

PA-42. Meetings of children at weekends.

As she had been notified at the previous meeting, she would be allowed to see her children on several Saturdays, in a house with outdoor space, with a huge vegetable garden that was well-prepared and perfect to allow the children to go for walks. However, going outdoors was subject to their good behavior. There was a spacious room for these meetings.

The mother usually brought food and toys. There were moments for them, where they remained in silence, moments of games. Always with the presence of the DT, one of the people who took care of the children and the IT as a linguistic support. The DT did her particular follow-up, with both parties present, asking about the young children's performance in general.

The mother was also given indications and asked questions about how she was feeling and other situations. The caregiver was quite serious, with a firm appearance. She was taking the encounter very seriously. The DT informed the mother that the next Saturday it would be her husband who would be able to spend time with the children in the same house.

As you might expect, there was also talk with the children, one of whom was not very young, although I must say he was not very talkative. Perhaps, being older than his sister, he had more knowledge and understanding that the situation he was in was not very comfortable, living apart from his parents.

In any case, the two were very calm and without apparent complaints, playing, moving around the room and enjoying the food that their mother offered them.

Taking advantage of the fact that the children were playing, the DT assessed their case only with the mother, asking for more details about her husband's behavior, she wanted to have a comprehensive report from the mother.

The mother repeated some of the comments already made, and was not very severe with her husband, although she made it clear that he had assaulted her and that the matter had been recurrent in terms of threats for a long time.

She valued the withdrawal of her children as something very negative for her. She missed them and felt a lot of pain for having them removed from her custody. She trusted that she would be able to get them back soon. As for their father also being able to see them, she did not comment, but simply shook a shoulder.

Later she made comments to me that she did not agree that the children should be taken away from her, she said, the behavior of the British was not correct, and that she thought it was other reasons, because although the husband had become somewhat aggressive, he had never touched the children, that has to be said.

The sessions were long, up to three hours. Finally, the DT agreed to allow the children to go outside. This is what the children wanted the most. It wasn't too cold, and it was 1pm, good weather to enjoy the outdoors.

PA-42. Dad's meeting with the children.

I also attended a week later, on Saturday (these meetings were always on weekends) to the new appointment, now with the husband and children.

The husband was most agreeable. He was showing his best face. He smiled with me (he thought that as IT he could make an assessment of these meetings (which is not the truth). He brought food, flowers, gifts, acted like a Papa Noel.

Whenever he was alone with me, he attempted to influence me by badmouthing his wife. The responsibility he felt he had in this situation, if it wasn't for her, he said, the children would not have been taken away from us. She was the one responsible for his misfortunes.

He was a really nice man during the visits. Active and conversational with all parties. It was hard to understand that someone like him could change to the point of assaulting someone in the family with a knife, but of course, cohabitation is another story.

To be honest, I had the impression from the first day that both the caregiver and the DT felt a strong inclination towards the father, they acted quite differently from the way they did when meeting with the mother. They were facilitating the meeting between both parties. They interacted more permissively.

The *modus operandi* was similar to the meetings with the mother, although the father's attitude made it easier to relax. They did the same things, trying to give the children time in the outdoor space as long as it was not raining.

I attended three such meetings on weekends, with each party, the mother and the father. After that, I never went back. I do not know how the matter was settled.

7. Cleaning the Scrotal Area

The two cases I am going to discuss in this section were performed in a private clinic. In all cases, it must be noted, the patient was always extremely satisfied with the results. Good feedback and, with no complaints of excessive pain or any negative connotations, no such reproaches were ever made.

A definition serves as a gateway to the first session with PA-08:

Vasectomy is a surgical procedure that a man can undergo if he no longer wishes to have children. It is a long-lasting (permanent) method of male contraception. Other methods of birth control must be used until the surgeon tests the semen to make sure there are no sperm left. This usually occurs about three months after the procedure.

PA-08.

PA would be about 35 years old, dark and with an athletic body, he was telling me that he had decided to have a vasectomy because he already had three children and did not desire to have any more (this is the most common reason why couples decide to take this step).

Since the first minute I noticed that he felt comfortable with my presence, and that he liked me. That calmed me down. He spoke with a lot of energy and was talking about his commute to the clinic by public transportation. He had a car but had not decided to use it because of the post-surgery, so he was going back home by public transport (bus). He was telling me about his home country, how long he had been living in Middle and other details that he thought it would be worthwhile for me to know.

The truth is that there were many clients in the clinic, more than in other times. The clinic also offered sterilization for women. Vasectomy, of course, was not the only specialist practice performed. We had been scheduled for 10.00 am, but the waiting time was significant, so just relax and wait.

The occasions when the time of waiting is long and the patient is already with the IT, are not always so comfortable. In this sort of clinics, and given the nature of the procedure, we are advised to be with the patient. On the other hand, in other cases, it is not only not advisable but not recommended. It is not always good that impasse of "friendly chat".

After about 45 minutes of queuing, the doctor called us. It was the specialist who was going to perform the procedure. His character was really pleasant, he communicated with ease, forcefulness of content and transparency, in addition, he allowed time to translate with solvency. Some clarifications that were indicated:

- During the surgery, two ducts called vas deferens are innervated and sealed. The vas deferens transports sperm from the testicles to the urethra. The urethra is the tube inside the penis. Once cut, the sperm cannot reach the semen or leave the body. The testicles continue to produce sperm, but the sperm die and are absorbed by the body.

A man who has had a vasectomy still produces semen and can ejaculate. But semen does not contain sperm. The testosterone level and all other male sexual traits remain unchanged. For most men, the ability to have an erection does not change.

Often, a man can resume sexual intercourse soon after vasectomy. But he must use another method of birth control. This is because some sperm may remain in the vas deferens for some time after the surgery. Another method of birth control should be used until the surgeon tests the semen to make sure that no sperm remain. This usually occurs about three months after the operation.

The DT kept going. Vasectomy is very safe, but all surgeries carry some risks. Some of the possible risks of performing vasectomy were also pointed out:

- An inflammatory reaction to sperm shed during surgery called sperm granuloma which can cause a tender lump under the skin.

- Epididymitis or orchitis (painful, swollen and tender to the touch epididymis or testicle) may occur after vasectomy. This occurs most often during the first year after surgery.

- Rarely, the vas deferens may grow back together.

- Prolonged pain after surgery.

Supposedly some of these issues have been explained before, although now with the help of IT.

DT: You may be wondering what the vasectomy recovery period is like. After a vasectomy you can:

- Return to work in two to three days.

- Resume normal exercise in seven days.

- Return to sexual intercourse in seven days.

The side effects were discussed, a direct explanation of the whole procedure was insisted upon, the relevant report was made with all the required details so that the PA knew for sure what was going to happen there.

There was a prudential waiting time and the procedure was carried out at once. Everything went very quickly, the PA-08 returned to the room and, with a gentle gesture of approval, took the mandatory rest time before leaving. There was cooperation and a good result. The nurse gave him the container to use to send the samples to the clinic to be checked by the DT.

In the meantime, he was reminded to use contraception until he passed the test to prove that his semen is sperm-free. The DT would inform him of this once the relevant tests had been received. The PA-08 made gestures of approval and understanding. The surgery was over, now it was up to him to give it a happy ending. After all, the samples could be sent by post, not the hassle of travelling.

*****

PA-43.

The patient had not yet arrived at the clinic when I first entered. I could see that the reception window was open, so I submitted my credentials. The lady nodded, checked my identity and invited me to stay because the PA-43 was on his way in.

I had been previously here so I sat comfortably knowing the process beforehand, something that always happened and, which gave me a bit of peace of mind, especially when it was so early in the morning and cold in winter.

More than 10 minutes had passed and I saw how a man came in, and just by the name on the card I guessed it was my PA-43. I was totally right, I introduced myself and we went back to the chair.

I was surprised by his very young appearance, maybe not even 35 years old, he spoke very fast and asked me questions. In theory, I told him, we had to wait for them to call us to give him the adequate and timely explanations, I was only the IT, so it was better to hold on. He understood, and didn't want to pursue the dialogue, he remained silent for a few minutes.

We were immediately called into the room where the doctor who was going to perform the vasectomy was expecting us. I informed the PA-43 what the documentation process was, several preliminary questions would be explained to him (although perhaps some had already been told to him before) but on this opportunity with the reassurance of the interpreter's assistance.

His mood was good, he did not seem worried, rather, resolute and hoping to finish as soon as possible. When I told him that between today (when the vasectomy was to be performed) and the moment of sterilisation there was a wait of a few months, he twisted his chin and asked me to explain this to him, because he thought that the process was completed and concluded at the time of the surgery.

The conversation became a little tense, because the doctor noticed immediately the point of the demand for explanations and said clearly that I should translate it very precisely that this question had already been discussed at his earlier visit and that no one had ever told him that the process was concluded with full effect on the day of the procedure itself. He had to choose a parallel means of contraception while waiting for the final confirmation of the DT.

No surprise to me, from the cases I had attended before, we can say that in 90% of the cases the same thing happened at this point. Only in this case, the PA-43 seemed really very shocked and a bit disappointed.

It is also true that the doctor was being much more severe, it was as if he was tired of repeating this question. For my part, I did two repetitions, made the situation transparent to the PA-43 and that was it. Little by little, things seemed to get back on track. My clarifications of the translation seemed to have convinced the PA-43.

The other details were made clear to him, time of surgery, whether he should take any painkillers, etc. It was also made transparent to him that for the next three months he would have to send a sample to the clinic once a month, by post, without the need to go to the clinic, he would be given a package and envelope to send it to the clinic when he left the procedure.

Once these samples had been received and after this short period of time, the doctor would contact him to state that everything had been completed, that the process had been concluded and that the vasectomy had come to an end. At this point, he would be able to have sexual relations without having to resort to other means of contraception.

It was pointed out to him that during those months he was still fertile, so he should keep in mind to use some form of contraception to avoid an unwanted pregnancy. Once he received final confirmation from the doctor, then the process was complete, the vasectomy took effect. In other words, sterilisation does not take effect until final approval.

I must admit that I had to repeat this question to the PA-43 several times, but I didn't mind because I realised that in this case it was really crucial to establish the situation, once the PA had been confused in the beginning. I should make it explicit, that a legal note is not bound here either.

I have heard of cases where a PA denounced the doctor because the vasectomy has no effect, and it is really because of this issue that a document has to be signed and hence a translator is called in for this task, which in principle should be very simple and straightforward, namely simply to inform the PA-43.

But regrettably it is not, there are almost often doubts and embarrassment or misunderstandings in this environment, at least in the experiences that I have been able to attend.

PA: Yes, everything is in place. It's all right. No problem.

We moved on to another hall already on standby to go in for the surgical procedure. There were several people in the room waiting. PA-43 was quite embarrassed, he might be thinking that he was going to be the only one.

I don't think they were all just waiting for vasectomies, or even for preliminary examinations, but one way or another we just had to queue for our turn, which according to the given info would not be for longer than 30 minutes.

The atmosphere was one of absolute well-being, the sensations felt good, the PA-43 was now calm again and, because of the time spent on hold, he began to talk about the reasons for his decision. Once again, I could not keep myself from having to listen to his personal matters.

His wife already had one child with another partner, she had been separated, and now with two more children together they were not even imagining the possibility of raising another family.

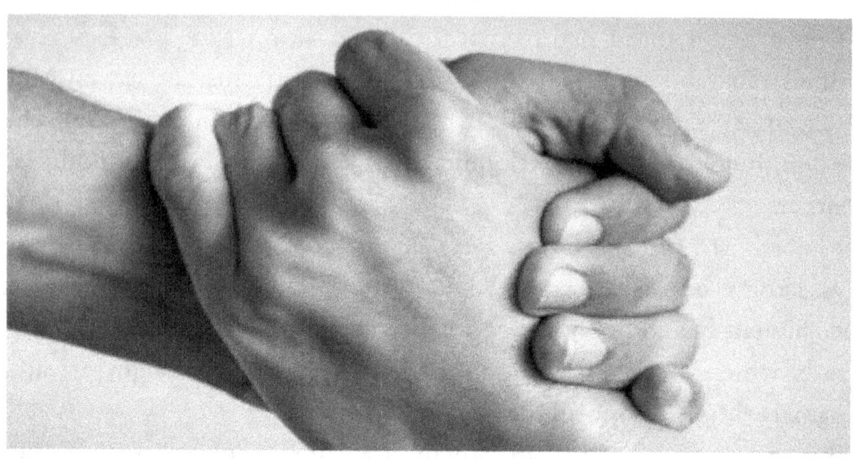

Vasectomy seemed to be the best option for them because, according to her, the contraceptive method used by her partner damaged her body and she did not feel safe keeping on with this method, nor did she trust its reliability in the long term.

For his part, he said, he was a healthy person and didn't want to give up sex with his partner, so he thought vasectomy was the way to go. I nodded, not saying much, trying not to absorb things too much, putting my mind elsewhere.

The intimacies of a PA-43 are not my concern, nor is it professional to get involved, but in these cases where the PA-43 expresses himself in this way, there is little to be done. I told him I was going to the bathroom and would be right back.

When I came back as soon as I sat down, he resumed his talk. It was as if he felt the urge to share all this with someone to get it off his chest, in reality I was no more than a stranger who spoke his language but whom he had just met a few minutes before.

I was quite astonished, because he went further and was telling me about the frequency of his sexual life and a few other things about his private relations, which made me feel a bit embarrassed.

I have to say that I found him to be a charming person who was only interested in finding a remedy to a family problem, or to put it another way, trying to avoid a potential conflict in the future derived from having unwanted children.

I tried to interrupt the dialogue a bit, I asked him if he was playing any sport. He told me that he joined a gym near his house from time to time, but that it wasn't something that excited a lot of him, that his preference was to watch sport on TV, and that he did do it regularly. The doctor gestured to us from the door of an adjoining room. It was our turn.

As you would expect in IT, I did not enter the surgery room, but this was a lounge for many patients, all of whom had already undergone surgery or were in the pre-operative phase, as was our case. Here the nurse gives a few last instructions, all very apparent, such as putting on a gown and little else.

The PA-43 enters the surgical room and I calmly keep waiting for him to return. Interventions are carried out quickly.

During the wait, that Woody Allen film came to my mind, where the director joked that he had become his own character in a scene full of spermatozoa that were going to be fertilised. I was reminded of a moment in a café, where, sitting with some friends, someone had brought up that scene in the course of a talk, which, simple as it was, was both humorous and surprising.

Everything was going smoothly. A positive look on the PA-43's face, even a smile. I must admit that I felt a very agreeable satisfaction to see that the PA-43 was completely at peace, that he had forgotten his doubts and that he must not have been in pain or anything of the sort, judging by his face and his fluent words.

Somehow I felt that my contribution had helped to make it all go right, even though technical intervention is not part of my personal baggage, of course. I only had one doubt, why the patient did not ask if vasectomy is reversible (maybe he had already asked in another session).

When departing, a short waiting period is requested before leaving the clinic. You are being offered something to drink, coffee, tea, milk, or other drinks, and they also have biscuits, doughnuts and some fruit. The atmosphere was friendly. Of course, IT may not accept invites.

8. Stroke Prevention and Analysis

PA-13.

A succinct start to the subject being quoted here: a stroke is caused by the interruption of the blood supply to the brain, usually due to a broken or obstructed blood vessel. This cuts off the supply of oxygen and nutrients, causing damage to brain tissue.

PA-13 had suffered the stroke while working. Now lying on a hospital gurney, she was in the process of recovery. According to the DT's comments, it had been very hard days of suspense. She was feeling fairly fit, moving with relative ease and speaking clearly, although without being exact, although she had one eye fully bandaged, the reason being that she had lost her sight (only in that eye).

The side effects of stroke depend on the part of the brain that is injured and the severity of the damage. It is essential that there is sufficient blood flow to the brain, a non-invasive, ultrasound examination of the brain. This test measures the speed or rate at which blood flows through the blood vessels of the brain.

At the beginning the question that needs to be asked:

DT: How are you feeling:

PA-13: Fine, I just have a headache and, a little bit, this eye.

DT: The one with the bandage?.

DT: Yes, the one with the bandage. And the other one?.

PA-13: No, the other one doesn't hurt, I can look fine. But I'm worried about the other one, I think it's going to be a problem, before the attack I didn't have any trouble.

DT: It's not surprising, because the incidence of the stroke has affected that eye, the doctors are working so that you can recover your sight.

The DT made it clear that we would follow up on the post stroke progress, given her language limitations she would also inform the doctors attending her of the outcome of this session in case what was said there was helpful.

She was queried about the medication, whether she was taking it regularly, and whether she was observing any noticeable positive effects or her feelings about it. Stunned at this question, she said that everything was fine, although her facial expression changed and she did not seem to know what to answer. The names of medications were mentioned, and the schedule for taking them.

PA-13 seemed to comply and was responding to the treatment, as could be deduced from the talk. She said that at times he would feel a sudden drowsiness after taking one of the prescribed doses, but that her headache would improve.

Another pill, he said, made her nauseous, but she had already told the nurse. The DT took notes on everything that was said and waited for my translation.

The next questions would be about her ability to fully recall her life before the stroke. Key point, because I had been informed that PA-13 had no memories of vital aspects of her life.

She was asked a series of private life questions, starting with the basic one of repeating her name (trying to discern if there was any memory loss). She was asked about her family, she hardly hesitated to answer, she was clear in the way she communicated the data.

The difficulty seemed to be when talking about her job. She didn't seem to be able to remember when she was attacked (which had been at her place of work) or what her job was, her reaction changed when she wanted to talk about it, she kept quiet and said that she did work there, but in a very vague way.

It remained that the clearness of thought that she had for other tasks was now turning into doubts, her brain needed time to sort out her ideas, and there was no straightforward answer. The DT noticed this, and tried to soften the questioning, because she didn't want PA-13 to become nervous or blocked in her attempt and effort to reply.

It was not easy to discern if the PA-13 could not remember or if she was not motivated, in fact some South American cultures often perceive this type of attack as something fortuitous associated with a strong emotional impact.

I kept thinking about an article I had read before starting the appointment about the symptoms of stroke. In it, there were some basic aspects of stroke, related to memory loss. Things and aspects such as the following:

A stroke can affect the way the brain understands, organises and stores information. This is known as cognition. Here we explain the different ways a stroke can affect your cognition, the problems it can cause and what you can do about it. It is aimed at people who have had a stroke, but also contains information for family and friends.

This is always enriching reading, it allows one to be closer to the process of translation as one assumes some of the outcomes of the disease to be both logical and commonplace.

You don't require to be a professional in the field, it brings you closer to the knowledge of the disease and makes it easier for you to interact with the parties present.

The NHS is really prolific in this approach, always with straightforward and plain content (explanatory brochures), with a large number of pages with tips about the most prevalent diseases.

The DT outlined some of the most common post-stroke side effects:

A stroke can be fatal. Among those who survive, many will suffer long-term disability. They will probably always need help to speak, move and care for themselves.

DT: Long-term complications of a stroke can range from (among others):

- weakness or lack of movement (paralysis) in the limbs.
- difficulty speaking or swallowing.
- difficulty reading or writing.
- changes in sensation to touch (sensory problems).

- changes in the way you see or understand things (perceptual problems).

- problems thinking or remembering (cognitive problems).

- problems controlling feelings and emotions.

These questions were running through my mind while the DT was giving a break between questions and a glass of water with a break. I don't know what the DT's intention was, but I must admit that in other cases I have participated in, the recognition queries were always asked quite quickly, as if not giving too much time for reflection.

These questions were running through my mind while the DT was giving a break between questions and a glass of water with a break. I don't know what the DT's intention was, but I must admit that in other cases I have participated in, the recognition queries were always asked quite quickly, as if not giving too much time for reflection.

I would assume that this is due to psychological therapy reasons which have been clearly prepared, I don't know, it might simply be a modus operandi of this DT. It is also presumably an attempt to prevent the negative states of the PA-13 such as supposed depression or suchlike. Here, as if listening to my inner thoughts, the DT continues to mention just this exact fact:

DT: I should warn that symptoms can lead to depression.

Symptoms appear suddenly and can include muscle weakness, paralysis, abnormal sensation or loss of sensation on one side of the body, slurred speech, confusion, vision problems, dizziness, loss of balance and coordination and, in some haemorrhagic strokes, sudden severe headache.

Full recovery is often achieved as the brain learns to compensate for the damage. However, many people never fully recover their previous abilities. Depression is common among people who have had a stroke. You may not feel motivated to take medication or complete physical rehabilitation.

DT: This can lead to changes in personality and mood, depending on which part of the brain is affected. This can be distressing for family and close friends. It is valuable to try to return to normal life as much as possible. Try to resume some form of work and engage in your favourite activities, hobbies and interests (as soon as you are discharged from hospital).

DT: This can lead to changes in personality and mood, depending on which part of the brain is affected. This can be distressing for family and close friends. It is valuable to try to return to normal life as much as possible. Try to resume some form of work and engage in your favourite activities, hobbies and interests (as soon as you are discharged from hospital).

We need to assess through sessions such as the one in which we are in, the signs or negative aspects in order to achieve improvement by targeting the weak points or by placing emphasis on relevant medication.

They are caused by a brief interruption of the blood supply to part of the brain. Because the blood supply is restored quickly, brain tissue does not die, as it does in a stroke, and brain function quickly returns.

The other 20% of strokes are hemorrhagic, due to bleeding in or around the brain. In this type of stroke, a blood vessel ruptures, interfering with normal blood flow and allowing blood to leak into brain tissue or around the brain. Blood that comes into direct contact with brain tissue irritates the tissue and, over time, can cause scar tissue to form in the brain.

I also remember reading in the same booklet in the entrance about "strokes" by nationality, where it was said that certain nationalities were more prone to have strokes. The DT didn't mention this at the time, I couldn't guess the nationality of PA-13 either, although her accent clued me in.

Blacks, Hispanics, American Indians and Alaskan Natives are more likely to have a stroke than non-Hispanic whites or Asians. The risk of having a first stroke is almost twice as high for blacks as for whites. Blacks are also more likely to die from a stroke than whites.

There were other issues, I mean physical deficits, that PA-13 suffered from that were already being assessed by his doctors at the hospital, but they were not the specific subject of our appointment.

Strokes usually damage only one side of the brain. Because most nerves in the brain cross over to the other side of the body, symptoms appear on the side of the body opposite the damaged side of the brain.

DT: The main modifiable risk factors for stroke are:

High blood pressure. High cholesterol levels. Diabetes. Obesity, especially if the excess weight is around the abdomen. Obstructive sleep apnoea. An unhealthy diet (e.g. high in saturated fats, trans fats and calories).

PA-13: It's true, the doctors have asked me repeatedly in the past few days about all these things you say.

DT: That's right, your medical records show all that follow-up.

******

PA-22.

It was a couple, the man came with a stooped air as if he was having a hard time moving properly. At first glance there was no visible injury. I had waited for them, there were only two people in the room and, as the chart showed that my patient was a man, because of the time of the appointment, I guessed that it was them.

As soon as they sat down, I stood up and greeted them, to check that I was indeed the person I was supposed to be giving translation support to. They confirmed that I was right. We quietly waited for a few minutes and then the doctor called out his name for us to come in. I instantly realised that they knew each other, that is to say, that they had had other appointments before. At first, the questions were the obvious ones, whether it was better and what was the purpose of the appointment, whether they were just coming for follow-up or for something in order. For my part, I had not yet been able to find out what the illness or disorder was.

The woman began to speak in a more energetic tone. She said that her circumstances were very painful, that he was in a lot of pain, and that they were finding it very challenging to cope with their life. The DT said that the surgery was still very recent and that the side effects were something that had been discussed and contrasted on previous visits.

The PA-22 knew that, yes, she knew that, but they were in need of something else, as the medication was hardly working. He had a lot of headaches, and they were very intense pains. He couldn't sleep. She commented that they didn't expect to face these pains after the surgery. She said that they had not been warned that something like this could happen, something so scary.

Then, she looked towards her partner (it was not clear if he was her husband or not), who nodded as he took off the woollen cap he wore on his head (quite usual at this time of the year as we were in the middle of winter). The truth is that although the man was the PA, he hardly spoke, the talk was between the DT and the woman.

Brain aneurysm repair is surgery to correct an aneurysm in or near the brain. This refers to a weak area in the wall of a blood vessel that causes it to bulge or balloon out and sometimes burst (rupture). Endovascular repair (surgery) had been performed.

The DT simply insisted that he knew it was hard, but that they had to be a little tolerant as giving him more doses of medication could impact him badly, he would be in bed most of the day for sure, and that was not good for the recovery process.

The woman listened, and became more nervous, she did not subscribe to the DT's opinion. She demanded a solution, she couldn't admit that her partner was in so much pain. Now she was reiterating to me:

- Come on translate (as if to speed up the conversation).

As if forcing me to translate faster. It was really very pushy. The DT was standing on the sidelines. Her husband kept quiet with his head down. I didn't mind her attitude, but it seemed to me that she was doing it with a certain provocative spirit. In these cases, with such a serious illness or surgery, the truth is that one can understand that there is aggressive behaviour, pain and annoyance.

So there is no choice but to put up with it and try to assist the patient, although no matter how fast the translation is done, there will never be any improvement in the PA-22. On the contrary, slowness is more suitable.

The truth is that PA-22 was still not calming down much, the DT told the woman that he was going to give her another prescription, that PA-22 should take the medication he was giving her but on the condition that she stopped taking another previously prescribed pill.

He asked them both to be calm and to rest, with self-control. I think that there was a well-defined recovery plan, which had been started in other sessions, because the DT always spoke as if they were things that had been contrasted beforehand (for me it was my first appointment, I don't know to what extent it was true or not).

PA-22 looked at me, accepted the new treatment option, but frowned, said things about it not being enough, and stared at me, as if he didn't like me very much either. I think he thought my translation wasn't helping him, he was looking for something else, my support to convince the DT of his points.

This scenario is a relatively common one, at times when the PA is immersed in a complex and painful medical crisis (with a lot of pain involved), he stops dealing with the IT as what he is, a translator, and acts with extreme pressure, as if asking him to be involved in the pain, or demanding that he collaborates and fixes the medical condition.

The session ended, we left together and I left, they didn't seem to be willing to say goodbye, which to a certain extent I appreciated. I can only wish them that the pain goes away.

******

PA-18.

PA-18 had been suffering from a stroke. She was no more than 40 years old. She may have been from a African country. She was accompanied by a man, I was not told who he was. I guess from the proximity, the way he held her hand and the way he addressed her, I suspect he was her husband. She was physically good looking. Again, no previous relevant data (for the IT).

Other stroke patients look like they are on the verge of death, she looked like she had just come out of a refreshing sleep. Everything smelled nice and there were flowers. On the sides of the room, small bunches of flowers of different colours, it was very cheery.

The question was that she had lost her memory, judging by the first sentences uttered by the DT.

There was a sequence of queries about her day-to-day activity in the scope of her memory check. She was very hesitant in answering, she took a lot of time, in this case the DT did not put any strain on the interview, everything was very gentle in the approach.

PA-18 had a very peculiar smile on her face, as if she wanted to use this smile to make up for some of the answers she did not remember, which were pretty simple. At least the smile was upbeat, even if it was not very expressive.

She said that what she did remember were the symptoms before it happened. She had experienced, sudden difficulty speaking (difficulty coming up with words and sometimes slurred speech), sudden confusion, with difficulty understanding speech, sudden dimness, blurring, or loss of vision, particularly in one eye, and double vision, sudden dizziness or loss of balance. Then it was as if I had a strong dizzy spell. Everything was a blur.

The husband stayed close, but did not interfere. Let's say he was offering his encouragement, but in total silence, fully understanding that it was the PA-18 who had to make the extra effort to reply with a view to finding out her condition and/or the progress of the disease.

Another visible side effect, one arm was affected. Partially non-mobile. The PA's gestures and position gave it away.

DT: Recognising and reacting quickly to the symptoms of a stroke is crucial for the successful treatment of the person experiencing a brain injury. Treatments for acute stroke depend on the time that has elapsed since the stroke episode.

That is why it is so crucial to promptly detect the symptoms of stroke and to act as quickly as possible. In the case of this PA-18, the disease had been immediately dealt with.

Now it was time to face the recovery phase. I must admit that of all the PA's I had assisted with this disease, it was the one with the best appearance, the best memory and the best recovery conditions. Always, of course, within the gravity of the disease and the options mentioned by the DT of being able to suffer another attack.

The DT also mentioned an MRI (I don't know exactly for what purpose).

If needed to confirm the diagnosis, a specialized type of MRI, called diffusion-weighted MRI, can show areas of brain tissue that are severely and usually permanently damaged and no longer functioning. Diffusion-weighted MRI can often help doctors differentiate a transient ischemic attack from an ischemic stroke. However, this procedure is not always available.

It would take a lot of hard work to get that arm back on its feet. Rehabilitation is started in the hospital as soon as people are physically able usually within 1 or 2 days of admission. Moving the affected limbs is an important part of rehabilitation.

Regularly moving the limbs helps prevent muscles from shortening and becoming tight (called spasticity). It also helps maintain muscle tone and strength. If people cannot move their muscles themselves, a therapist moves their limbs for them. People are encouraged to practice other activities, such as moving in bed, turning, changing position, and sitting up.

Look at what the NHS leaflet said about this disease as a summary:

- Modern treatments for ischemic and hemorrhagic stroke have reached an advanced state of development in the modern era of digital and device technology.

- Neurointerventional treatments enable surgical procedures in the brain without the need to open the skull surgically and provide excellent treatment alternatives for all forms of stroke and cerebrovascular disease. These developments are timely, occurring in an era when stroke incidence is on the rise as the population ages.

******

PA-71.

I was not informed of the exclusive reason for the visit. There were three people, a man, a woman and a young man. Although I had no information, I was able to figure out that someone in the family had already suffered a stroke, I think he or she was an inpatient.

They were going to be briefed on the prevention and after-effects of these cases of stroke, connecting with the one suffered by their family member.

Look at what is said in this *practice point* of the Practical Guide for Psychologists (APS):

- Doctors inform interpreters about the nature of the consultation before it begins, whenever possible, recognising the need to help the interpreter prepare for the information he or she may have to interpret. But in most cases, mainly the more complex and challenging ones, no information is given at all, making the task harder for the IT, especially in these cases where the theoretical burden is very high.

The DT was alone, on the medical side. It was an office of a private clinic, although there was no noise or other people, the room was locked, so at least we could have the meeting in calm. It was not my first time in this clinic, hence, I had some idea of what we could deal with, and is that whenever I went to this clinic was for issues of stroke, cases most of the time the state was quite serious.

The DT started the lecture. He did it as if it were a conference, he had a screen and a projector. These kinds of things were said:

The 80% of strokes could be prevented by acting on a small number of risk factors, such as hypertension, diet, smoking and exercise. Preventive measures would also contributes to a massive reduction in stroke and to the overall targets for reductions in cardiovascular disease, cancer, diabetes and other major causes of death and suffering in Middle.

It would also facilitate a focus on two very key points of support:

- Access to low-dose combination therapy for patients at medium risk of stroke.

- Access to innovative mobile technologies to facilitate access to preventive information.

The DT showed at the same time some images on the screen, which she could at times use to go back to them and what they meant, or, at other times, simply leave them as an explanatory visual reference. The attendees showed interest, listened to my translation and followed the process devised by the DT.

He also displayed details of the 2018 UK Stroke and Transient Ischaemic Attack Guidelines for Stroke Prevention in Patients with Stroke and Transient Ischaemic Attack. The guideline was really complex, it presented a lot of varied background material, with specific terminology, and she offered a link in case those present wanted to review it later.

It reflected a section she had entitled "Warning signs, risk and prevention of stroke". There are several warning signs of a possible stroke:

- Sudden numbness or weakness of the face, arm or leg, on one side of the body.

- Sudden confusion, difficulty speaking or understanding others.

- Sudden difficulty seeing out of one or both eyes.

- Sudden difficulty walking, dizziness, loss of balance or coordination.

- Sudden severe headache with no known cause.

He also reiterated that prevention is always a beneficial factor. The best way to keep the brain healthy is to prevent a stroke from occurring. The best ways to keep a stroke from occurring are the following:

- Keeping blood pressure under control through lifestyle changes.

- Do not smoke or stop smoking.

- Take measures to control cholesterol.

- Limit alcohol consumption.

- Exercising regularly.
- Maintain a healthy weight.

The speech was very well arranged, it was in powerpoint, the data was very concise with images and strong arguments and messages. The audience seemed to follow the reasoning and did not ask questions.

The doctor can prescribe medication to treat pre-existing conditions that can affect the risk of stroke. Follow these guidelines:

- Ask for a refill two weeks before your medication runs out.
- Keep taking your medication even after you feel better.
- Talk to your doctor about medication-related side effects.
- Tell your doctor if you are taking any over-the-counter medications.
- Use a pillbox to organise your medications.

Also, she was talking about habitual medication. Some were mentioned broadly, such as antiplatelet agents, drugs that help prevent blood clots and reduce the risk of myocardial infarction or stroke (possible side effects include increased risk of bleeding and easy bruising).

Aspirin/dipyridamole (Aggrenox), Clopidogrel (Plavix) or Ticlopidine (Ticlid), or anticoagulants (blood thinners), which reduce the blood's ability to clot. Possible side effects include increased risk of bleeding and easy bruising. Dabigatran (Pradaxa), Heparin or Warfarin (Coumadin).

Food and proper diet were listed as measures to prevent stroke, moving on to a more specific warning: manage stress. As we feel more stressed, our blood will be producing more hormones. Although useful in small amounts, over time an excess of these hormones can damage blood vessels and lead to hypertension.

Many life events, such as moving house, losing a job, family problems, can be stressful. Everyday hassles can also cause stress. There are many forms of stress. Identify what stresses you and learn to manage it as best you can.

The DT reminded those attending of the causes of high blood pressure. In their case, there was a very strong factor that they should never forget: family history.

Stroke interrupts blood flow to the brain: without oxygen, brain cells die. Is a form of cerebrovascular disease, meaning it affects the vessels that supply blood to the brain. Like the heart, the brain's cells need a constant supply of oxygen-rich blood.

*****

PA-25.

As at other times, the patient was not entirely sure why he or she was going to do the test, but had consented to the doctor's guidance. This always poses an additional complexity for the IT, because translating this type of statements is not easy to convey when the PA-25 is not entirely certain about the reason for the test. In a way the IT becomes a go-between who makes the story easier to explain and makes the facts more explicit.

The woman arrived with a smiling face about 20 minutes before the appointment, I was waiting for her. She was accompanied by another woman. We introduced ourselves to each other.

The session was for a pre-medical screening, prior to a Transcranial Doppler (TCD) Ultrasound. This laboratory had a Transcranial Doppler Ultrasound which is used to measure the adequacy of blood flow.

As usual, the PA-25 would be informed in detail about the specifics of the ultrasound, the test set-up, what happens during the test, after the test and the overall procedure. This patient spoke almost no English, so the work of the IT was even more necessary.

This non-invasive study is performed by highly qualified and experimented neurologists and technicians with special training in neurovascular ultrasound and experts in stroke treatment.

DT: How does the TCD works?. The TCD sends sound waves through the skull to the arteries. The sound waves, called ultrasound, bounce back to give an indication of blood flow in the large arteries of the brain ("speed").

The sound waves hit the red blood cells (RBCs) in the blood. These sound waves change the velocity of the RBCs. The TCD records their intensity when the sound waves bounce back. The difference in intensities detects abnormalities in blood flow to and within the brain.

DT: What will happen during the test? A neurovascular technologist will instruct PA-25 to sit in a chair or lie on a bed. Gel will be applied to different areas of the scalp to prevent air bubbles from blocking the sound waves, as ultrasound does not travel well through air.

There are usually three areas of the head examined: the temples, the closed eyes, and the back of the skull. The technologist will adjust the volume of the loudspeaker sound to locate the blood vessels to be studied. The test usually lasts between 45 and 60 minutes.

PA-25 had listened to the DT. She was a mature woman, her age was hard to judge, she was sitting motionless, observing me with curious and appreciative eyes. She was accompanied by a relative, who was in charge of the rhythm of the discussion. It was all very private, I mean personal.

This transcranial ultrasound was done because of signs such as loss of balance, frequent weakness in arms or legs, tingling or numbness on one side of the body, chronic migraine and a family history of stroke.

DT: What are the uses of TCD?.

- Diagnosis of narrowed or blocked blood vessels and arteries supplying blood to the brain (carotid artery stenosis and occlusion).

- Detection of patent foramen ovale (PFO) and other orifice(s) of the heart that did not close as they should have after birth (shunts).

In this case the overall TCD application explained quite succinctly and, I admit, I had to ask her to repeat twice, in order to proceed with my task. The family member stared at me, seeming not to like me pausing. For the DT this was not a big problem.

For my side I respect the patient's demand, but I must also make it transparent that nobody commented to me in advance what it was about, no guidelines were given to me nor a preliminary that is supposed to be given in cases of manifest complexity such as this one. The IT needs a briefing, particularly in these cases. There was a lot of terminology.

If one of the parties is hard-nosed, or let's say very pushy, the talk can take on tinges of a mild tension that should not be there. The fact that the IT asks for it to be repeated, which is a common scenario in regular discussions, does not reflect a lack of knowledge, but rather the opposite, it signifies a desire to concretise the terms and carry out the translation work as professionally as possible.

On the other hand, the level of demand in this meeting, based on the speed of the discussion, can be detrimental, it is about explaining and facilitating to the patient basic points about a single procedure, the details, it is not about doing it with a stopwatch in your hand.

And there were more explanations (among others):

- Detection of vasospasm (constriction of a blood vessel) following haemorrhage in the area between the brain and the thin tissues lining it due to haemorrhagic aneurysm or trauma (subarachnoid haemorrhage).

- Monitoring of drugs that dissolve blood clots (thrombolytic therapy) in blood vessels to determine the occurrence of Reperfusion (tissue damage).

- Monitoring of cerebral haemodynamics (blood movement).

There were no comments on medical history, nor on medication, everything was focused on TCD. Finally, mentions of procedure data:

- Safe and painless, no complications, provides immediate results, patient can leave after the procedure, procedure takes approximately 45 to 60 minutes.

This was the only case I attended of this nature, I mean TCD. This is one of those cases that leaves a bad taste in your mouth. You don't know why, there was nothing unusual, and the atmosphere was like so many other times, but I felt uneasy.

The lack of prior knowledge is something very serious, it can end up damaging the IT's in a short space of time, no matter how much experience and dedication they have to do their job. I took a train back from Pancras station and my mind was returning to its original mood.

PA- 33.

PA-33 experienced a sense of being frustrated by a missed achievement, a strong personal desire to achieve that particular goal had led her to a very emotional hardship. She regarded herself as frustrating in this regard and, for a long time, this negative feeling had been going around in her mind. She was asking the DT for help in dealing with these very negative thoughts.

PA-33: When I least expect it, the same memory comes back to my mind. That day I find it very problematic to concentrate on my duties and my mood drops abruptly.

DT: Does it influence your routine?. Do you have an energetic life?.

PA-33: There are phases when I am active and those emotions are put aside in my mind, but suddenly they come back, particularly in those bedtime or waking moments, as if it were a nightmare. It's always the same thing.

DT: So it also affects your rest?, your sleeping times?.

PA-33: Not always, but the days that it comes back, my mind absorbs it completely, I wake up like from a bad dream, although I know which dream it is, but it's hard for me to go back to sleep.

DT: What do you do when you wake up?.

PA-33: I simply drink a glass of water, or go out on the terrace for a few minutes, after a short space of time I feel better. The thing is that it happens again and again, as I said, in short intervals of time. I have the impression that my temperament has changed for this reason. I find it much more harder to laugh, it's as if I'm afraid of myself. I am more hesitant to express my feelings.

DT: Laughing can be a good outlet for these moods. At best, it stops internal tension transiently or mitigates anxiety and excitement for a few moments.

PA-33: It's not just the dream, the problem is that my mind goes to that downside too often, I feel that I have failed myself, that my mental abilities are in doubt. The fragility comes over me, I feel I have no control over myself.

DT: In reality, a missed achievement is just that, a single missed achievement, you should try to set other goals, and that way when you achieve your new goals the wounds will disappear.

Your unfulfilled desire is harming you, because it feeds on the lack of something you don't have at that moment, even something you may have lost so long ago that you have forgotten it and are left with only the emptiness that the loss left behind.

PA-33: I have been even resorted to taking sleeping pills, but that doesn't improve the condition much, although I have to admit that the pills are indeed working, but I fall asleep very easily during the day. They are prejudicial to my work. The sleep doesn't last 24 hours, during the hours I don't sleep the condition comes back again and again.

DT: Who prescribed you those pills?.

PA-33: The GP doctor.

DT: I understand. Are they efficient?.

PA-33: Yes they help you sleep, but they don't really help the big picture.

DT: Desire is the source of your suffering because it enslaves you. When we are obsessed by a thing, the possession or enjoyment of it becomes for us an absolute urge, and greed is a source of torment. Not being able to satisfy the desire produces the frustration you are talking about.

The sooner you learn to use limits to your advantage, to accept frustration with awareness and tolerance and to make discipline a value, you will overcome it. You need to learn to manage it, to guide that feeling.

Desire is urgent and pressing, it seeks to be satiated if possible quickly, or better still, instantly. And it drives us to action in haste to achieve, at whatever cost, what we desire. That is why it is so important to find ways to learn to manage impulses and desires, as well as to understand and train frustration tolerance.

PA: I don't know, I don't see myself with much strength to achieve the discipline you're talking about.

DT: You cannot give up and you will realise your wildest dreams. Otherwise, frustration can become a very destructive emotion for you. In fact, it is already doing that job, you have to stop it.

DT: You have to block that major feeling of discomfort. Instead of following that dynamic, you should spend some time thinking about why you haven't achieved what you wanted so much and you will find the best alternatives. Set yourself a new goal or goals that are real.

By setting yourself a real objective, you will combat your level of self-demand, it is like a brake, time has passed but you feel worse and worse, set yourself the real objective and go for it, you need smaller goals, that will be the brake. That will help you for sure to achieve better physical and mental health. Focus your efforts along those lines.

*****

PA-11.

PA-11 said that he had recently arrived from his home country a few weeks ago and that since his arrival he had been feeling very unwell. He had constant chest pain and a general malaise, with severe muscle pain, trouble sleeping and strong contractions in his legs, mainly at night.

PA-11's appearance was ghastly, he really resembled someone who slept in the street, he smelled disgusting, that smell of some homeless guy who lives in the underground and sits next to you. He spoke very slowly, but with a consistency, and, very quickly, he had me up to speed on his pains as soon as he identified me as his IT.

He had come from an African country, that he had been given a contact by some friends to come and that they would give him a job when he arrived, the trouble was that there was no one at his friends' address, or rather, his friends were not there, and now he was worried about his future, how to settle in decently and how to face his job search.

To make matters worse, his health difficulties were striking him hard, but he was glad to come to the doctor and was hoping for remedies in the next few days. His look was clear and direct, he communicated with great ease.

He was always very fatigued and he was touching his left side of his chest, at the level of his heart. The DT said that they were going to do an ECG and explained the reason.

An electrocardiogram can be used to measure or detect:

- Irregular heart rhythms (arrhythmias).

- If blocked or narrowed heart arteries (coronary artery disease) are causing chest pain or a heart attack.

- If you have had a previous heart attack.

- The effectiveness of certain heart disease treatments, such as a pacemaker.

You would need an ECG if you have any of the tracking signs and symptoms listed below:

Chest pain. Dizziness, lightheadedness or confusion. Palpitations. Rapid pulse. Shortness of breath. weakness, fatigue or decreased exercise capacity.

DT: An electrocardiogram (ECG) is a simple, non-invasive test that records the electrical activity of the heart. An ECG can help diagnose certain heart conditions, such as abnormal heart rhythms and coronary heart disease (myocardial infarction and angina pectoris).

We moved on to the ECG, later the doctor would ask him further comments and questions, but he wanted to have the results of this ECG. PA-11 lay down on a stretcher and the doctor installed the devices for reading the ECG.

Deprived of the clothes on his upper body, the doctor could see that his skin was marked, at first it reminded me of someone who had measles, the DT's question was obvious, as she wanted to know where the dreadful condition of the skin on his chest and back was coming from.

Her answer was quick and blunt. It was that in the old room in which he had stayed, there were fleas on the mattress and while he didn't realise it, they had bitten him for several days causing what could be seen. Red marks of different sizes were all over his body.

The PA-11 was asked to lie down on the stretcher. The doctor cleaned several areas on his arms, legs and chest and then placed small patches called electrodes on those areas. The total number of patches was not stated.

The DT asked him to remain immobile during the procedure. She also asked him to hold his breath for a few seconds while the test was being performed. It is important to be relaxed and warm during ECG recording, as any movement, including shivering, can alter the results.

If symptoms tend to come and go, they may not be detected during a standard ECG recording. Your doctor may recommend remote or continuous ECG monitoring. In this case it is not requested.

The patches were connected by wires to a machine that converts the electrical signals from the heart into wavy lines, which are usually printed on paper. The doctor reviews the test results.

Those lines represent the electrical signals coming from the heart. If the test is normal, it should show that the heart is beating at an even rate of 60 to 100 beats per minute.

Many different heart conditions can show up on an ECG, including a fast, slow, or abnormal heart rhythm, a heart defect, coronary artery disease, heart valve disease, or an enlarged heart. An abnormal ECG may also be a sign that you've had a heart attack in the past, or that you're at risk for one in the near future.

The ECG result was quite negative and confirmed the suspicions of DT. The patient showed signs of tiredness and fatigue, asking if it would take long. At that time the doctor was in a separate room so I could not confirm.

DT: Are you a smoker?.

IT: Yes, I have smoked for several years.

I told him that they would do other specific tests. But in your situation he would have to apply for admittance to the hospital immediately.

10. Stiff Muscles and Slow Breathing

PA-40.

I was very surprised by the PA-40 due to her appearance, she was young, this was not usual in this category of cases. She was in back pain and in strong pain. The DT gave a longer than average feedback on her problem. Often, osteopaths are quick to take action, this is a practical application, but today he turned a twist.

The young woman said she was very dissatisfied with the therapy so far. The DT was acting more distant than usual (I sensed that he might not believe her complaints). In any case, PA-40 gradually began to relax and lay down on the stretcher, as the DT asked her to do, even though she was wincing in pain.

I kept my distance, I didn't need to be close to them to translate, and I didn't want to be in a space that could obstruct their movements. This session was in an indoor room, quite large. I mention this because most of the time, they are done in spaces that are only separated by curtains, but today it was otherwise. The room was really comfortable.

The young woman, as she lay down before the DT touched her, asked me to translate where her painful area was and that she had twinges and pain when she turned around and things of that nature. These comments did not seem to surprise the DT, who had treated her before. The PA-40 was showing an unusual insistence in her complaints, physiotherapy PA's generally listen more to the DT and follow the exercises looking to maximise the session, today, however, with this PA-40 it was different, she was not acting very participative, at least at the beginning.

It could be said that she was afraid of making movements that would cause her more pain than the one she had when she came to the clinic. The PA-40 said that she didn't know if it was the muscle strain, the ligament strain, or whatever it was, but that there had to be some inflammatory process for her pain not to stop. She couldn't figure out how the constant check-ups didn't work. There was no doubt that the PA was approaching the risk factor of anxiety.

From feedback, his type of ailment was long-standing, and she had been on the lookout for the right therapy for long time. On the other hand, X-rays and other scans had found nothing out of the ordinary, no serious injury, hence the DT's doubts. The picture was a bit misleading, I mean the PA-40 mentioned pain in the leg.

The DT was saying that leg pain is mostly caused by compression of the sciatic nerve with muscle contractions, sciatica is one of the common complications of back pain, but rarely in people of her age, but rather in older people. This should be checked in depth.

The DT applied the techniques using his hands and gave guidance to the PA to perform smooth and precise movements following his indications. The PA performed only part of what was requested and then she immediately said that she was in a lot of pain.

There were several exercises demanded by the DT, always with a partial ending. The DT asked her to try again after a few minutes, simply to relax and try to follow the steps indicated.

Most osteopathic techniques are quite gentle and aim to correct mobility and balance. The osteopath carries out a diagnosis which entails assessing the degree of freedom of movement in certain joints in connection with the patient's back complaint or pain.

He seeks to recover the body's lost balance, re-activating the self-healing mechanisms through diverse therapeutic techniques. Osteopathy is one of the branches of physiotherapy that treats a large part of the most common musculoskeletal pathologies.

With the application of the muscle energy technique, the DT attempts to relax pensioned or shortened muscles. The patient performs a sustained muscle contraction while the therapist stretches the muscles. There was a question from the DT about the application of another technique, but the patient in this case flatly refused.

Interpreting physiotherapy sessions requires a good knowledge of terminology of the human body, musculature and bones in the setting of multiple pathologies. The presence of IT is not always well interpreted, we may need to refer to a APS *practice point:*

Doctors introduce the interpreter to the person and explain the role of the interpreter as a non-clinical member of the healthcare team, who has the task of facilitating communication in the clinical consultation through interpretation, while maintaining impartiality.

I fully agree. Although this practice point is oriented to different options with doctors and PA's, it is particularly valid in physiotherapy appointments.

******

PA-100.

The doctor told me to come in, as soon as I introduced myself as an interpreter. The room had toys in it, as if it were a children's ward.

DT- It's a case of asthma, in a child. I called an IT, because the last consultation they didn't understand anything, they have just arrived in Middle and neither of them speak English, neither he nor his mother, and they are on their own. I can give you some general tips if you want.

IT- OK, tell me in a general way some things about the disease.

DT- Yes, look, you can also use this PC by doing a search. Yeah, sure, there's all the wisdom there (referring to the search engine).

While the DT started talking, I listened to her and also did a search on the PC, with short phrases like: Is asthma spread?, can I transmit it to my children?, or similarly, so that I could also compare some of the definitions with her and apart from learning something new, I could use up the waiting time of the PA that was running late.

Here are some intriguing details that popped up on the screen, and which were fully embraced by the DT:

Asthma is not "contagious" because it is not an infectious disease. However, some people think it is because:

- you can catch a cold, which can make asthma worse.

- asthma and allergic conditions often run in families, and some people think that asthma is an infectious disease.

- asthma is more common now and people believe (wrongly) that the disease is spreading as an infectious disease.

The DT adds some worthwhile insights:

One of the strongest plausible explanations for the recent increase in allergic diseases is the so-called "hygiene hypothesis". This long-standing theory claims that people exposed to many different infectious organisms are protected against the development of allergic diseases.

IT- Can asthma be cured?.

DT: No, asthma cannot be cured, but it can be controlled with effective treatment. Symptoms can be completely relieved with effective treatment, and can sometimes disappear even without effective control. Asthma is therefore a volatile disease. There are times when people think they must be cured because they are completely asymptomatic. Although this symptom-free state (called remission) can last for a long time, once you have had asthma you will always have the risk of having it again, even years later. It is probably better to think of asthma going into remission rather than being cured.

IT- Can children die from asthma?.

DT: Children can die from asthma, but it is very infrequent. However, when a child's death could have been prevented, it is tragic.

I read in the local newspaper that someone had died as a result of an asthma attack. Why does this happen?.

Because asthma is so widespread, it is easy to think that it is "just asthma", but it is essential to know that asthma can have very serious repercussions. Although deaths from asthma are rare, many of these sad events are associated with potentially preventable factors and therefore could have been avoided.

Many deaths occur in people with uncontrolled asthma, so it is vital that you have regular check-ups, especially if you need to use more than one reliever inhaler per month.

There was a knock at the door. In entered the PA-100 with his mother. The PA, or rather the mother, took the disease very seriously, she did not fall into the usual error of regarding it lightly, as a mild disease, on the contrary, she asked, investigated and queried and wished to obtain all the necessary information to update the improvement or future forecast of her son.

DT: To prevent asthma attacks and possible death:

- Have a personal asthma action plan (ask your doctor or nurse for one).
- Take asthma seriously.
- Make sure you regularly pick up prescriptions for preventive inhalers.
- Take your medication regularly.
- Go for asthma check-ups.
- Find out how to tell if your asthma is out of control.
- Seek urgent medical help if your asthma is out of control.

You have very severe and unstable asthma despite taking your asthma medicines. It is fragile asthma or severe chronic asthma.

PA-100 had been rushed to hospital days ago. His asthma was causing him serious health complications. The DT also insisted on preventive inhalers.

******

PA-65.

The drop-in was in a modern, high-capacity centre. I was directed to a room that looked cosy and quiet. There was a bed and an elderly woman was in it. At first she did not seem to be moving. I was given some very generic notes on her condition and little else. Two members of the medical staff came in at once.

The old woman looked in very poor health, as far as I could observe. She barely moved and did not seem to say anything or respond to the initial comments that were made, which at the moment were not directed at me, which aroused my curiosity as to what kind of translation I was going to do under the circumstances.

I was instructed that we would be expecting a daughter and son who were on their way in. We waited a few minutes and, sure enough, a woman arrived, and I was also told that the son would be away, so we could begin. The last of the medical team to enter was the doctor, very young and energetic in her expressions.

She queried if I was the interpreter, although I had been introduced, of course, and I said yes. She frowned and, I got the sense that she didn't approve of my being there, she looked a little disapproving. It was as if she had been introduced to a cat.

A paramedic made it clear that the patient was under the effects of a strong painkiller, which had been administered just before our arrival. The others who were present remained silent, including the daughter, who was the last to reach us.

I became a little embarrassed, because the old woman did not say anything, only slightly wiggled two fingers on her right hand, but did not talk. I was seriously beginning to wonder why I had been called as IT, and how I was going to be able to maintain communication with someone in this state.

The DT would take the initiative in questioning, continuing with a rather energetic and almost belligerent tone, in contrast to the silence and little action from the other people present. The daughter was sitting near the bed, holding one of PA-65's hands.

The DT was reviewing the patient's state very quickly, barely giving me time to translate for those present. She pointed out that the daughter understood the language quite well so I didn't have to worry about her, the key point being that I had to repeat to the patient everything that was said there in her native language (said the DT).

This remark confirmed to me that the DT did not approve of my presence. To say that I had to translate into the original language of the PA sounds like a joking matter, that was my job and that was the task that was always done, there was no point in having to do it all over again.

I nodded, although I did not fully grasp DT's words, she refused to repeat herself and what she said did not make much sense, because the old woman did not really say anything, she could only utter a soft babble like that of a child who does not know how to speak or of a newborn baby.

Her posture on the bed was fixed, static, there was no movement at all except for the wiggling of the fingers of her right hand. At times some of the fingers of this hand did twitch, but she was not even able to move the entire hand.

The daughter kept looking at me, but she was completely silent, not saying a word. The others stood at the back of the bed and observed, but did not say anything either.

Then the DT began a series of questions addressed to the PA. I did the respective translation and kept waiting for the patient to answer, but as expected, nothing at all, it was like asking random air questions.

The scene was becoming really embarrassing and grotesque for me, as I had never been in a comparable predicament before. I was thinking of conveying my displeasure to those present, but ultimately I decided to move on, hoping that things would go in the right direction.

The DT asked up to five continuous points and, after each one, kept looking at the PA, waiting to see if she was going to answer. The old woman said not a word, her eyes were open, but there was no movement in her voice or words.

For my part, the position was very difficult to maintain, it was very obvious that the old woman was not in a condition to co-operate because of the medication, she could not communicate (I don't know if she would have been able to do so without having received the painkillers).

To my major shock, the DT asked me in a rather unpleasant way if my translation was good, if I really knew how to speak the old woman's language. Nobody said anything, the query seemed to me out of place and far from what a medical professional should do.

Firstly because it valued my skills in a manner that is totally inappropriate, assuming that my level of language was the cause of the old woman's failure to reply. The point was that the poor woman could not manage to speak. I even had my doubts whether she could really hear what was being said in there.

I wondered if she really knew what she was talking about and what her motivation could be for such an extremely aggressive attitude towards myself from the beginning and, seeing clearly that the patient was totally inert, her body was not responding, she was an old woman completely under the effects of the medication. To my absolute horror, the rest of the attendants did not say a word, no one said anything.

Two more questions were asked, all by the DT. The old woman remained the same, nothing had changed. The questions were interestingly aimed at finding out whether the elderly woman had the decision-making capacity on vital medical aspects and choices to be made in the next few days regarding the future of her illness.

Concretely, there were some points that emphasised the idea of whether or not she wanted to undergo surgery. It is presumably an attempt to verify whether or not the PA could decide for herself whether or not she wanted to undergo surgery.

The fact is that my case was at the limit, I was not informed at all about the PA's illness, I was not provided with any information about what the meeting was about or what the objectives were, I was not given any details about her medical history, and I was judged that my task was not well done because the old lady was not responsive.

The doctor went back to the battle, she said that my translation was not accurate. I was absolutely perplexed, said nothing, and looked at the others, seeking their opinion, but no one said anything. I tried not to address the DT directly to avoid conflict, it was hard to understand her valuation of the situation by focusing on me as a failure.

It was all very weird, trying to communicate with an old woman in that state was out of the question, unless she was mute (no one had told me she was). The doctor was speeding up and trying to carry on with a meeting that was essentially a monologue, her own particular monologue.

She kept saying things to the others, that for her it was the last meeting and that she would make the opportune report and comments to promptly indicate the progress of the PA-65, but that she was very sure of the steps to follow (without mentioning them).

I walked out of the room as quickly as I could. I presented my personal assessment of what happened to the agency. I hope that the old lady will recover and that she will be able to voice her thoughts to the doctors, because otherwise this meeting would have been absolutely useless.

It was very definite that knowing, as the paramedic had indicated, that the PA had received strong painkillers minutes before, the appointment should have been cancelled at once and a new date proposed once the PA-65 was in a stable condition, not under the effect of such strong drugs, then it would be possible to verify with neutrality whether or not she had the capacity to make the decision about her surgery.

It would have been worth knowing the doctor's CV, whether she had been in practice for months, or days. Her knowledge of the organisational and management aspects of this nature of appointments was null and void.

Her nervousness appeared from the beginning, damaging the entire scenario, her attitude towards me was illogical and inexplicable (if she thought it was not valid she should have said so in the first place, cancelled and asked for another IT), besides, how did she evaluate that my work was badly done if the person involved, the PA, did not speak. On the other hand, why didn't those present (including the daughter) say anything at all?.

If you are reading these lines, ask yourselves for a second, if you were in the shoes of the IT, what would you do?. How would you react in such a case?.

******

PA-57.

It was not the Centre for the Elderly with individual rooms, I think it was for the elderly but also for disabled people of other age groups with different severe physical handicaps. The fact is that PA-57 had his own independent flat, that is, in a building, with special assistance and specific conditions, but with an independent living quarters.

He was an aged person, I don't think much older than 60. He had serious mobility problems, in a wheelchair, but with options to walk on his own slowly with his crutches, although he could not stand for a long time, the propensity to fall was apparent.

I was not given a medical analysis or feedback either, so I do not know precisely what his physical sequelae were, the degree of impairment and how they had been caused, whether simply by age or wear and tear. In some way, in my view, he appeared to have been injured by an accident. He was living in his flat, which he showed us in passages, but he had a lot of obstacles to access the bathroom with a guarantee of total autonomy, both for the basics that need not be mentioned, and for hygiene and showering habits. She often needed the support of a carer, as she could easily fall.

The physiotherapist's aim was to instil mobility techniques in him, which would help restore his ability to access his basic physical functions with complete flexibility and autonomy.

We accessed the toilet, he was given advice on how to enter, how to fix his body, what postures he could adopt to facilitate mobility, how to use two metal bars embedded in the wall as a support. All with the physio's assistance. At times the PA-57 showed anger at not being able to do almost exactly what he was told, but his reaction afterwards was very positive.

It is amazing to see what can be achieved and progress can be made in this regard, simply by changing the habit of moving the body or managing the speed of a particular movement.

With practice, confidence and, with the proper strict adherence to the advice of a good physiotherapist, this level of improvement can be achieved, which not only gives a PA-57 confidence in their physique but also in the psychological realm.

I say all this, as I could see after three repeated visits, in short periods of time, more or less once a month, how the PA-57 improved mobility substantially.

We must recognise that he was a very optimistic man and with a lot of emphasis on following up on all the advice he was being given. I

was surprised that being so active he had so many language barriers and needed IT.

Generally a person with this level of energy, who had arrived in the country years ago, would worry about having an average level of language skills. He, on the other hand, needed IT for the most crucial instructions.

He had a huge TV screen, in front of which he claimed to spend most of the day watching his favourite series. The walls were painted sky blue. There was a lot of light outside, a large window at the top marked the temperature, which was pleasant in contrast to the cold outside. The atmosphere was cozy and warm.

The dimensions of the flat were not very spacious, but it included all the basics, kitchen, bathroom, bedroom and the living room where I watched TV, and a small storage room. A small flat, but complete, especially for a single tenant (no one said if there were other tenants).

It was obvious that the PA-57 liked to chit-chat, the talk flowed quickly and I was constantly having to translate. Everything became more relaxed, and we moved on to the physiotherapist's instructions.

We moved on to focusing on the real objective of the visit. We reviewed the whole process of routine housing movements, which, although tricky, considering her physical condition, he seemed to have learned well and had no adaptability complications.

The physiotherapist was more inclined to be more focused on making his movements in the bathroom more effective. On the ground, he was told how to handle the shower. He was supposed to have succeeded, i.e. he could do it by himself using the area in question like any other person (his bathroom had adapted conditions).

He was being instructed on strict movements, how to be cautious and other specific questions which the physio insisted on with absolute precision and, in which the PA listened to me when translating with utmost curiosity. I have witnessed comparable cases where the PA does not respond willingly to the guidelines and suggestions, in this case it was quite the opposite, the PA was collaborating 100%.

The session had its dynamism, and before I knew it, almost two hours had passed. At other times it is a bit tiresome to follow up on these visits from my position, but in this case the time had slipped by quickly. The date of the next visit remains to be confirmed.

The physio had the appearance of being really satisfied, it was obvious that the PA was improving his mobility.

It was Christmas time. On the way out I could see the Christmas lights that had been put up in a department store across the street, with a very funny Santa Claus at the main entrance. I felt the need to put my gloves on my hands because of the cold weather, and I followed my footsteps down the pavement in search of my next booking.

PA-66.

It was a bit of a struggle to find the ward where this appointment was to take place. The hospital was very huge, and I had never been in that area before. With the help of a nurse I was able to sneak into one of the waiting rooms, full of patients, and in a short time I was able to find my PA-66. A young girl, I reckon in her early 30s.

I kept my cool, in hopes that she would tell me something about the subject at hand, or just that we were waiting for the call from the DT. She was looking a bit nervous.

Then we would have to go to another flat, because it was a case where a payment had to be made. The process would have to be paid for by the PA-66, it was not cost-free.

She had requested this consultation shortly after her arrival in Middle, because she feared she had breast cancer. She didn't explain very explicitly if she had been tested in her home country or how she had made the determination, but the appointment would be along those lines, she wanted to know whether or not she had breast cancer.

First we had a theory session, this is to help detect the problem's origin, which is called diagnosis.

DT: The symptoms of breast cancer that PA-66 developed were basically:

- Redness or scaling in the nipple or breast area.

- Sinking of the nipple or pain in that area.

- Pain in the breast.

I had heard many things about breast cancer affecting older women, menopausal, post-menopausal, obese, women who had never been pregnant. In this case I was particularly surprised that the girl was quite young.

The DT talked about various aspects, some of them personal, she also mentioned the need to familiarise oneself with the breasts during a self-examination in order to become aware of the breasts. She also spoke about preventive medication and surgery.

Finally, she was indicated that she would have to pay for this process, the amount to be paid, and we were told on which floor the office was located and who she had to ask to carry out this step.

She requested payment from her boss, they had discussed that he would pay her, but she did not know the real price until she came to the hospital, so she messaged the boss, he would make a transfer on the spot, check the bank's app and she could go and pay.

The young lady persuaded the DT of this issue, so they would do the "tissue" test and she would agree to pay the processing fee a few minutes later. I thought they were very nice about allowing these payment options, in other cases they require payment in advance, otherwise no progress is made.

We spent a long time on some benches in the corridor. It was very close, and she was pretty nervous. She made contact with her boss, but it had to be by message because he had told her that he would be working and he preferred her not to call him. So she did and he replied that he needed an hour later he would transfer the requested amount.

The hospital was in full swing, the corridors were crowded with staff and patients moving back and forth, and there were many stretchers everywhere. In this hospital it was always crowded, no matter which floor I had to go to, it was very busy in all sections.

In the meantime, we went up to the floor where the office was located to make the payment. She explained the situation to him, I did my translation, and an immediate invoice was generated for her, which she would pay in cash. She described how she was going to do this. She would just wait for the transfer, make a cash withdrawal at the Hospital ATM and pay in full, 100% of the cost.

Then we went to a room, on the same floor but through several corridors. The person in charge of the test was waiting for us. She had all the data from the PA-33 and knew what she had to do. A few quick directions were given and they went to the stretcher.

I was very far away, at the entrance door. In this case, the DT suggested my position, which, although a bit far away, seemed correct to me. The PA-66's voice sounded good, and, although I had to raise my voice a little, I was able to translate fluently.

There wasn't really much to say, mostly comments, where the DT clearly informed PA-66 of what he was going to do to her. He was going to extract a piece of tissue from one of her breasts, as I said before.

I suppose that in order to keep PA-66 from moving, he climbed on top of her belly, I'm not sure but I could see a strange movement towards the top of the stretcher, I presume it was to avoid any sudden movement from PA-66.

It was all very fast, there was a soft whimpering sound, but it didn't go any further. I can't say for sure if there was also an injection. As you can well understand in these cases, I try to stay as far away as possible, my only interest is to help with words, nothing more.

The method was to remove tissue from the breast with a small incision (cut) in the skin to remove some or all of the suspicious tissue. The DT had reported that in this case there would be incision.

Often a small metal marker is left at the site within the breast so that the suspicious area can be easily identified on future imaging tests.

DT: The biopsy sample goes for analysis to a laboratory, where experts determine whether the cells are cancerous. A biopsy sample is also analysed to determine the type of cells involved in breast cancer, the aggressiveness (grade) of the cancer, and whether the cancer cells have hormone receptors or other receptors that may influence treatment options (as long as it is certified that cancer is present). Most people who need a breast biopsy do not have cancer.

At the end, PA-66 told me that it had hurt a little more than expected. But she was fine. I was sure it was going well. Her face was now a little more serious than when we first met, but she seemed very serene. There were no tears on her face.

On the way out, she checked her bank app, and signalled me the deposit she had received. Before, I had a meagre 30$ in her account (she had made a point of showing me the app page, it was an on-line bank used by foreigners living in Middle at the time, I had seen many of them pay with their brightly coloured cards in various shops, cafes and others: Monzo). Sure enough, she already had the deposit. Now she could pay for her session.

She was happy, she said that her boss was a very reliable person and that this was like an advance on her salary and that she was glad that he trusted her because it gave her encouragement and confidence for the future to work with them for a long time.

On the other hand, it gave her relief from the point of view of her health, although she would have to wait for the results, but without the help of her bosses she would not have been able to pay these expenses.

She told me that I had been helping her for a long time, now I could leave, she just had to withdraw the money and she knew the payment office from our previous visit. In fact, it had been more than two hours. She thanked me for my help. We said goodbye. Although I didn't tell her, I wished her test was negative. She was very nice and friendly, she deserved good news.

******

PA-13.

When dealing with a session with a cancer patient, the psychological skills of the IT (interpreter) are essential, not to express anxiety or distress is the key to a long-term assistance, not everyone feels safe to talk about such a serious health condition in the eyes of a strange person (even if he/she is a language support).

With cancer patients, our work sheet did not contain any data, no full names, no age or personal details. Sadly, once again, there was no briefing. Nothing at all.

PA-13 had received the diagnosis, breast cancer had been detected. Treatment after total breast removal course. She was an adult, dark-haired, light-eyed woman, about 5'5" tall, weighing about 70 kilos, with a kind smile and a clear mind. She was wearing black shoes and jeans.

DT: Although self-help techniques can be a good way to cope with negative emotions, it is nevertheless valuable to know when you might need more help. We all have bad days and crappy days, but it becomes a bigger concern when it starts to disrupt your life, your working life, your relations or your workplace.

PA-13 has undergone cognitive behavioural therapy (CBT). CBT focuses on changing the way we think and behave, and teaches coping skills.

PA-13: I have used various counselling. CBT and mindfulness-based mental health support programmes to help me stay on track.

PA-13: I still wonder what could have caused the illness.

DT: DT: Breast cancer is a complex disease and it is impossible to identify a single cause. We don't fully understand why some people get breast cancer and others do not.

The conversation was warming up. Although she remained serious and calm, the PA now seemed more confident in expressing her feelings.

PA-13: Cancer motivated me to switch my life. I didn't want to go back to my high-stress profession. The big shifts at work pushed me to withdraw. I have been maturing a lifestyle that suits me. Positive things can come out of hard circumstances, and life is for living.

As far as I could understand, it was like a review of his life over the last few months, because it had been quite a while since he had attended this specific practice.

DT: It is important to remember that you have suffered a serious trauma and that it is difficult to go back to the old life. This life, your new life, is the main thing, the new sense of 'normality'.

The conversation was closing, names of treatment came up, such as letrozole, sodium clodronate, etc., and there was talk of finding additional info.

It seemed that PA-13 was actively seeking drugs in addition to those provided by the DT and was asking around, which did not displease the DT, but was influential for her.

******

PA-27.

PA-27 had been diagnosed with cancer (bowel) a few weeks earlier and the purpose of this appointment was to settle whether or not he would agree to undergo surgery, as he had been very hesitant about it in a previous consultation and had asked the doctor for a short period of time to make a final choice.

He related PA-27 how he had made a short visit to his country of origin, had visited several relatives and how he had returned with the firm idea of going through the operating theatre. That's right, he agreed to the surgery that had been recommended to him.

The DT nodded and repeated to PA-27 that it was a total success because the disease had been detected in time and that meant that the chances of achieving good results were a reality, always within the context of the seriousness that the context of the matter involved.

PA-27 had a serene and calm face, he had attended the consultation accompanied by his wife who remained seated in a chair next to him.

My work was easy to handle, both they and the DT spoke in short, well structured sentences, with pauses to allow for good two-way communication. They seemed at ease with my visit.

Bowel cancer is cancer found in any part of the large intestine, which includes the colon and rectum. It is one of the most common types of cancer in Middle.

Surgery would be then performed to remove the cancer from the bowel, and some or all of the bowel around the cancer.

DT: To facilitate your post-operative recovery, you may need a colostomy or ileostomy, which may be temporary or permanent. You will be supported by our team of specialists during the entire surgery and recovery.

******

PA-29.

It was 14.30pm, the appointment was for 15.00pm, I was tired that day, I had arrived on time and I sat down to wait for the patient. It was a clinic outside the usual working area.

The work sheet did not specify any data, only that it was a "practice session", no names, no diseases, age or anything like that. I had the feeling that it was a confidential case, of seriousness or whatever, as absolutely all the details were omitted, only the place and the time.

The person who attended me in administration, not far inside her window, made a gesture to me at about 14.45pm, indicating a person who was sitting near me. It was the patient PA-29.

He was a man, maybe 65-70 or older, robust, well dressed, as the Middle area requires, and very talkative. As soon as I introduced myself as his IT, he embraced my presence with kindness and understanding.

When these scenarios arise, I introduce myself and wait for the session with him, although I try to avoid familiar chitchat, just to find out what it's all about and be better suited for the session. In this case, it was hard to keep my distance, because he was very talkative.

With hardly any hesitation, he explained to me that he had attended before, once a month he received a treatment injection and that was the reason for this new visit, and that he himself had never had a IT before, he thought that surely the doctor had realised his language barriers, which was why he had required the services of a IT, to expedite the session.

He had been detected with prostate cancer, these regular injections were the treatment he was receiving as, he said, it had been detected "early".

It was 15.05pm and we were called by the DT. PA-29 kept talking nonstop, at first I thought he was angry or upset or something, but then I realised that it was really his character. With the DT, he was complaining, saying that he didn't enjoy the side effects of the treatment (he was referring to comments that had been made in previous sessions) and that the injection was a bit painful.

The DT argued that he should not complain, that the treatment was cost-free, that in few countries would he find such facilities, that if there was a little pain he had to put up with it, and that he was very lucky because it had been detected early enough to follow the treatment and that this gave him a better chance of coping with the disease.

The DT was not English. She looked very professional, everything she said was absolutely fitting for the situation she was referring to, she moved easily around the room, around her table giving her particular explanations, and then came the question of whether he was ready and prepared for the injection. She took out her utensils and went about preparing the injection.

PA-29 didn't give any approving response, just kept talking about personal things, how the medication was affecting him, and that he was actually a little upset. The DT, however, went on with the preparation and didn't pay much attention, although she always kept waiting for my translation.

It didn't seem to me that PA-29 was upset or irritated, but rather, I think that the conversation and the non-stop talking gave refuge to a gentle tingling that ran through his body, I mean that nervousness that sometimes creeps up on us when we know that something might hurt.

The PA-29 was trying to interrupt her every time she switched several sentences in a row, he didn't wait for me to translate. But he was very nice, he was doing it with a very polite, witty air, I don't know, it seemed to me that he was attempting to get closer to the nurse, I think he liked her, and he didn't hide his feelings.

Doctors cannot predict how long hormone therapy will inhibit the multiplication of prostate cancer cells in an individual. Therefore, men who receive hormone therapy for more than a few months are regularly tested to monitor the level of PSA in their blood.

DT: Rising PSA levels indicate that the cancer has started to grow again. If the PSA level continues to rise even though hormone therapy keeps androgen levels very low, it means that the prostate cancer has become resistant to hormone therapy.

When he injected, he pulled back the curtain, as is logical, and said nothing while he was injecting. She did it relatively quickly, the truth is that the syringe, of a good size, contained a large dose of liquid to be injected. The DT pulled back the curtain, ending the injection, and smiled a gentle grin of complicity (as if pleased with the result).

The PA-29 had just got dressed and turned to me, saying that this didn't have to happen and that things should be different (I translated although I have no idea what he meant by these words), I think he was looking for a point of complicity on my part, I don't know, something in that vein.

I have attended other similar sessions, I mean with punctures and normally they are quick, in this case, dealing with the ailment in point, and the character of PA-29 it was lasting a bit too long, compared to the others, but I was satisfied, I mean that the translation and the contact with the client seemed to have pleased both parties present (or at least nobody said the opposite in my presence).

I offered the sheet to the DT to fill out, and I left. PA-29 came out with me, kept talking about how I was going to get home and so on. There was a fact sheet with details about prostate cancer in the waiting room. PA-29 asked me if I could please translate some of the pages for him. So I did. Here are some of the paragraphs:

Your thoughts and feelings. Changes in your body and sex life can have a big impact. You may feel worried, dissatisfied or angry. There is no right or wrong way to deal with these changes.

Some men may want to try different treatments for erection problems, and others may prefer to find other ways to be close to their partner. The important thing is that you find a solution that is right for you, and that you ask for support if you want it.

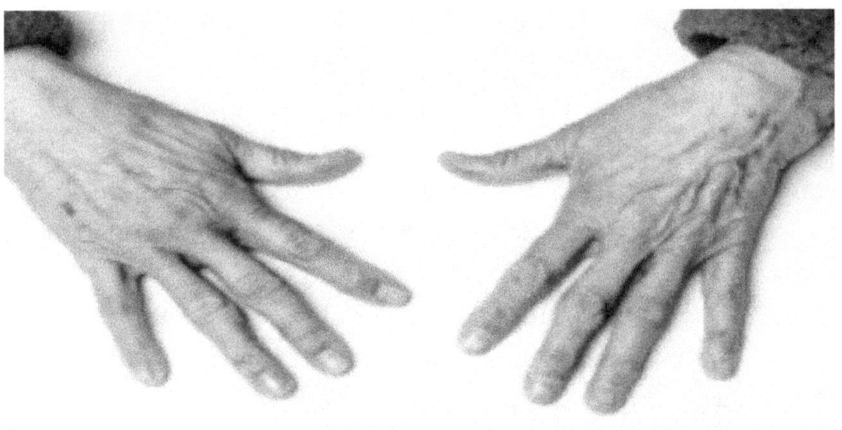

When should I start treatment? You can start treatment for erection problems when you feel ready. Starting treatment soon after prostate cancer treatment, for example with a low-dose tablet once a day or a vacuum pump, may improve your chances of getting and keeping an erection later on. If you already have erection problems, you can start treatment before prostate cancer treatment.

If you are on long-term hormone therapy, you can ask your doctor or nurse about intermittent hormone therapy. In this case, hormone therapy is stopped when your PSA level is consistently low, and restarted if it starts to rise. Your sex drive may improve while you are not on hormone therapy, but this can take several months.

The brochure was quite comprehensive, including explanatory photos of injections, implant options, different perspectives on the disease, and much more. It also suggested basic and relevant questions to ask the doctor or nurse, such as:

- How can prostate cancer treatment affect my sex life?. How long after treatment can I masturbate or have sex?. What treatments for erection problems would be best for me?. Can I get them on the NHS?. Is there anything I can do to prepare before I start prostate cancer treatment?.

- What if the treatment doesn't work?. Are there other treatments I can try?. What other support is available to me?. Can my partner also get support?. Can I get support?.

After the consultation I usually avoided contact with the PA, this particular one was very friendly and offered to take me for coffee in a nearby café, I thanked him, but stated that I had to leave immediately because I had another booking at a distant hospital. He nodded, shook my hand and said goodbye, thanking me for my help.

I think he talked a lot out of nervousness, because he was a really nice person, who was obviously worried about his complicated illness and his treatment. Everyone gets over their nerves in such a way.

It's one of those cases, where you feel complicity with the PA-29, I wish I could tell him not to worry, in a few days he'll be fine, it's nothing, but it's not true, because prostate cancer is a very serious condition that can change a person's life. So, I extended my hand, and I said goodbye.

12. Hard-to-Accept Moods

A procedure specified in the BPS, which will serve as an opening for another new case:

Before starting to work with an interpreter, it is worth bearing in mind any legal responsibility they may have towards the interpreter in relation to their psychological well-being and the criteria for a formal debriefing (after the consultation-debriefing).

This responsibility should fall on the agency providing the interpreter. However, it is nevertheless good practice for the psychologist to look after the interpreter's psychological well-being and to offer a brief informal discussion after the consultation with the client.

PA-91.

I attended several cases of this nature. About 75% of the patients were Brazilian nationals, now living in Middle, who suffered from this problem during the winter period.

Questions from the doctor:

DT: How are you feeling?.

PA-91: Very bad. I don't go out of the house.

DT: Do you have a regular diet?

PA-91: I eat chocolates, doughnuts and pills.

DT: Do you still live alone?. PA-91: I live with my mother.

DT: Have you been on medication?. PA-91: Yes.

DT: Have you ever felt like hurting yourself?.

PA-91: Yes, I have thought about throwing myself from the fourth floor. I don't know, I don't feel comfortable talking about it.

This case of PA-91 was particularly sensitive. He had attempted suicide by cutting the veins in his right hand (wrist). The wounds were not very deep, he had simply got dizzy and then woke up to go to seek medical attention (this had happened months ago). She was now under treatment and regular supervision. His mood was depressed.

In fact, he had been diagnosed with Seasonal Affective Disorder (SAD). In this case, the translating task was simple, I mean that the easiness of his mood favoured the slowness of his words and that did not create any complications. He was a very sensitive person, no doubt, and, wanting to be helped, he was willing to open his mind and heart to receive help.

The doctor pursued with further in-depth questions and made it clear that treatment (medication) was the key to improving his mood and temperament. I tried to translate as best I could and even repeated the sentences so that there was no room for doubt.

The look on PA-91's face was one of assent, and the DT regarded his expression with mild concern but with confidence that his work would be successful.

Common symptoms of this major depressive episode included:
- feeling hopeless or worthless.
- losing interest in activities they used to enjoy.
- trouble sleeping.
- experiencing changes in appetite or weight.
- feeling sluggish or agitated.

There were more suggestions, notably in terms of medication. The most commonly used drugs to treat SAD are antidepressants. Bupropion (Wellbutrin) mainly increases dopamine levels, while selective serotonin reuptake inhibitors (SSRIs) and serotonin-norepinephrine reuptake inhibitors (SNRIs) mainly increase serotonin levels.

PA-91 was concerned about one point above all the other problems arising from it, that of lack of sleep.

DT: Lack of light can disrupt the circadian rhythm. This can trigger the brain to produce too much melatonin, the sleep hormone, and release less serotonin, the brain chemical that affects mood. The result of this chemical imbalance?.

You feel sluggish and lethargic. Other common symptoms of SAD are lack of sexual energy, overeating (mostly from cravings for carbohydrate- and calorie-rich comfort foods) and social withdrawal (you said yourself you don't even step out of the house).

Both agreed that SAD does not only impact on mood. It is also connected to impaired cognitive function, such as problems with poor concentration and working memory (e.g. difficulty remembering newly learned information or finding the right words when speaking).

PA-91: Should I take an afternoon nap?.

DT: If you feel like it, why not, so we can counteract the lack of sleep and rest at night.

PA-91 told me, once the session was over, about his origins, the area where he grew up and how his trip and stay in Middle were not turning out as rosy as he had planned because of the SAD. I did not see him again, I did not have the chance to attend another session. I am sure he must have improved.

*****

PA-10.

PA-10 was going to a psychological consultation for the first time. His face was flushed and somber. The therapist introduced himself and made it clear that, as this was the first visit of PA-10, some points had to be settled beforehand. Hence the need for a solid translation.

PA-10 had requested this service through his GP (NHS), who saw that his medical help was not enough. The shock was immense, when a few minutes into the session, PA-10 started to cry like a small child, barely able to pronounce a word.

We took a break. As soon as he seemed more relaxed, the psychologist decided to resume her questions.

The main difference was that the psychologist asked PA-10 to specify what he expected from this session and from a treatment with her in the future. Or in other words, what she was asking, what he would expect from her. It was apparent that PA-10 was confused, did not know what to say, and gave the illusion that he had attended the session with his mind elsewhere.

Little by little he became more focused and elaborated on what he perceived as clear discrimination against him at work and how several of his colleagues were making his professional life miserable and were pressuring him to leave his job.

The psychologist again insisted that she understood the employment context, but that if he could not demand a specific outcome from her, she would hardly accept him as a regular patient.

The point is that in these cases, the IT feels the impulse not to remain in the sole shadow of the translation and to voice its opinion. To be fair, PA-10 was in need of help. But my job is other and I have to be as professional as can be.

The DT, made an impasse. She left some forms on the table and asked PA-10 to take 10 minutes and, with my help, answer these boxes. The idea was to discern in a broad way whether discrimination in the workplace was deepening depression.

DT: When employees face discrimination at work, there is not only the one-off emotional cost of a particular incident or set of dynamics. It can also lead to:

Clinical depression. Lack of commitment. Lower productivity. Feelings of isolation. Dehumanisation. Abandonment. Other negative consequences for physical and mental health.

DT: Discrimination in the workplace is widespread, and there is a clear link between discrimination and depression.

There were several explicit survey questions on the form related to these comments, with ratings from 1 to 10, and PA-10 had to choose the one they felt was closest to their mood, while giving it a value on that scale. The DT decided that he was going to switch strategies (in my opinion). She asked PA-10 to reflect on the issues discussed and that he would schedule another session in a week's time, at which he was hoping to settle the required points and thus set up a regular therapy, which was estimated to last for an initial period of three months (without saying how many sessions).

In my perception, the DT wanted to state whether PA-10 really wanted to keep the job or whether, because of his doubts, he had decided to quit. On the other hand, if there was depression, it was clear that the need for medication was necessarily present (PA-10 had said that he never took medication for depression).

There was also the fact that the psychologist had doubts as to whether it was depression or whether PA-10 was really trying to take advantage of the therapy for a work-related purpose. These were reasonable doubts for a first session, although the reality was that the man seemed depressed, down and unmotivated (in his own words).

For the moment everything was up in the air. The session was scheduled for an hour and we had already spent almost two. On leaving PA-10 tried to chat with me outside the consulting room.

PA-10 (Second session). A week later, while reviewing a petition for IT, I looked at the data in the file and see that it is the same person as last week. I attended this new session of PA-10.

PA-10 arrived with fresh thoughts. He had transformed his adversity. Why do I say this?. Because now he knew how to approach the DT about his basic goal for attending therapy. He said that he was afraid that his personality would change, that he would not be the same as before, once he was in this discriminatory context at the workplace, he asked the DT to assist him in therapy in this sense. The DT listened to PA-10's argument.

DT: Aspects of our personality can change for better or for worse over time, depending on many factors, the people around us, the people around us at work can be one of them. In any case, I don't see very strongly the relationship between the discrimination in your job, which you told me about last week, and the fact that consciously or unconsciously your character is going to change because of this reaction.

PA-10: Yes, but, all this is hurting me, I used to be a very outgoing man outside of work and now I've become much more closed off, it's harder for me to trust the people around me. And the worst thing, the last few weeks, I see that my wife notices, we used to get along with each other very well, I think it is also influencing my family ties. This is not healthy for me (PA-10 was talking and clenching both hands nervously).

The DT kept explaining that people don't move from being extroverted to introverted from one day to the next. He might have been worried about his business dealings and, obviously, that was changing his mood or way of coping with real life, but in itself, that did not mean that aspects of his character.

PA-10, said that he understood his words, but that until now he had never had these feelings, that he was a person with a stable mood, with good and bad days for sure, but that he had never required aid, but now he had the clear perception that everything was falling apart.

He urged the DT to support him in this matter, at work he would try to manage the pressure so as not to lose his job, because, he said, he thought that the aim of the harassment and aggressiveness of his colleagues was to get him to quit and resign. This was the only reason he could find.

PA: I need someone I can trust.

One of the biggest factors in the success of one's mental health journey is their level of comfort with their provider. Employees who are experiencing depression need a therapist who truly understands their experiences, background, and culture.

PA: I will talk to my manager again, but this time very seriously, I will tell him that I want to report discrimination at work. I will be direct and clear. Even if it won't help me, I will have a basis to defend myself legally in the future. I will use whatsapp and messages (so I can save them), so I will have proof that I have contacted him. If he still won't listen, I will hire a lawyer. I have to protect my rights.

We have a whatsapp group and I'm going to block it because they send hostile comments. He has to listen to me, if not at least I will have proof, I will be able to follow a legal route.

PA: The manager is supposed to take a firm stand against both internal discrimination and more generalised discrimination, and he should demonstrate to employees that he cares about our lives outside work as well, and improve psychological safety at work. he should demonstrate all these things.

DT: It isn't the individual employee's responsibility to change a discriminatory culture. There's only so much one person can do to push back against discrimination when it's ingrained in the workplace.

DT argued that personhood changes are forced by the social environment or, more accurately, by the need to adjust one's behaviour (and thus one's personality) to social psychological demands or to the norms and standards of society. In other words, we all have to adapt if we want to get along with others, keep a job or be responsible parents (for example).

PA: Yes, OK, whatever you say. But, if I lose my job, because of peer pressure, not because of my lack of commitment, because I work hard and well, I say if I lose my job and, on top of that, my personality changes (in my years) what is my future going to be.

I know that being in a foreign country has its difficulties, but after the years that I have been here, I don't know, I do feel defenceless, I have always had a lot of confidence in the local laws, but now I don't know where I can turn.

DT- To be frank, personality changes are not drastic in most cases. A person may become more or less introverted or conscientious, as the case may be, based on the events and experiences life throws at them. On exceptional occasions, however, there are those who manage to move from one side of the trait spectrum to the other over time.

PA-10: Sure, but I don't want to be one of those "rare cases". Why should I have to change my personality?. They're the ones who are playing me falsely.

He even thought it was a matter of racial discrimination because they had hired three more people a few months ago, and they were of the same nationality as four others who were already in his work group, it was as if they were rejecting him simply because he was of a different nationality, he had tried to talk to the manager, but he wouldn't listen to him.

PA-10 remains in the same posture, sitting to my right, sometimes moving his hands in assent to his words. He also looks at me, seeking sympathy. I translate and try to lower my gaze.

PA-10: Besides, I've consulted a lawyer, if I lose my job now, I'll be at risk after several years of work of losing some benefits in view of my retirement. I don't know, anyone would say that this is not a random thing. I don't know what to think. My approach to these people at work hasn't changed, I've always been the same, it's their behaviour towards me that has changed.

DT- A question: can the attitude at work be motivated by a promotion?.

PA-10: What do you mean?.

DT- What if your colleagues see you as a rival for promotion at work?.

PA-10: No, I don't think so, we are all in a somewhat analogous boat, we are not studied people, we do manual work, we have had a local manager for a long time, it has never been a problem, besides, I have no plans for promotion, I am happy with what I have, the only thing is that the conditions have worsened and I don't want to lose what I have.

I sometimes wonder why PA's who have been in Middle for a long time don't speak the local language. Many people have been in the country for many years, but they hardly speak the language because as they do manual labour, they just go about their daily work from a physical point of view and don't bother to improve the language.

The psychologist was quite young, maybe 35 years old, and apparently much more satisfied with the state of affairs in PA-10 than she had been last week.

******

PA-05.

The session started very strongly, the DT was moving from one side of the room to the other, with an out-of-character nervousness. She would touch her hair and turn to us. She was an unsettling woman, I thought that was fine and we were safe from disaster.

The comments were leaning towards the side of anxiety analysis, I would say if I had to choose a headline it would be something like: How to get rid of anxiety?. PA-05 was worried about the number of negative feelings she was experiencing in the last few weeks, talking about sudden mood swings. The DT had decided to pause.

DT: Negative emotions per se are not problems to be fixed or avoided, but are part of the range of emotions we all experience throughout life. We cannot choose what to feel. Negative emotions are just normal responses that need to be acknowledged, not avoided or denied.

In other words, we have to "feel comfortable being uncomfortable", because only then can we figure out what to do about the underlying cause and move on with our lives (Acceptance and Commitment Therapy (ACT)).

PA: The bad thing is when I'm sleepy, for example at dinner, then I fall asleep, and when I wake up my mood doesn't improve, I feel afraid, I don't know, I have trouble even deciding to go out in the street.

DT: That's certainly a challenging question. Nobody wants to feel sad, scared, lonely, anxious, exasperated or intimidated. Accepting life's difficulties, big and small, real or exaggerated (as they often turn out to be) and making room for discomfort in our lives is the healthiest path.

The more willing we are to experience difficult or painful thoughts and feelings.

The dialogue between psychologist and patient was really fluid, certainly they must have met in other sessions. PA-05 listens to her advice and waits for translation, although at times she gives the impression that she understands a sentence or two.

For my part, I did my best to complete my duties as firmly as possible, in the expectation that the psychologist's advice would be of real help to PA-05. Oddly, they look at each other, listen to my translation but barely look at me.

DT: When we make room for both bad and good experiences, we will eventually be able to embrace whatever difficulties life throws at us and learn from them what we can. It is not about overcoming our fears, but about living life to the fullest in spite of them.

If we tell ourselves that "we will try", we give ourselves a way out or a ready-made excuse. If we do, it is as if we are setting ourselves up to fail. It only works if it is absolute and unconditional.

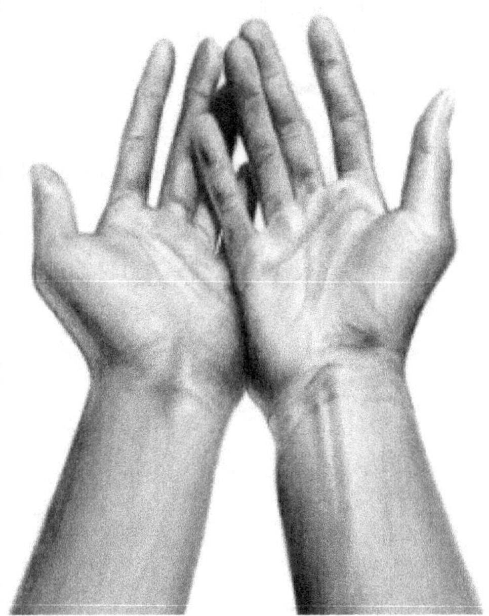

PA-05 remained calm, answered in short sentences and gave the psychologist the option of reviewing notes on her laptop which I guessed came from previous sessions and which insisted on the counter-analysis of events experienced and presumably overcome by PA-05.

It was such a personal statistical incentive, to prove to the PA that she could achieve if she put her mind to it. Some on-line sessions were also proposed if she preferred.

On other days, when I have to handle and translate these talks, it requires special concentration, perhaps because I am not having one of my best days, but on this one it went smoothly and, I must admit, so far I was satisfied with the result (as far as I was concerned).

Psychological dialogues are always a tricky business and require a very calm and coherent state of mind in order to avoid any omission in the translation or any form of personal judgement.

The image would be as if we were conducting the session in a complete empty underground tunnel, the two of them would be sitting a few meters apart in front of each other, while I would be 4-5 meters away, transcribing the talk out loud and going around in circles, I was on hand, I was doing my duty but it was as if I wasn't there. Yes, it was a fantastic, strange day.

*****

PA-06.

PA-06 said that it all started because she was trying to be pregnant. Her idea was that she had to find a partner by going out at night to party in a downtown area. She joined a dance club in the city centre. She made friends and, as she needed a job, she agreed to work as a hostess in the same nightclub.

The pace of the work was tough, especially as he had never worked at nightime before and it was very demanding from a physical point of view.

She started taking extasis. She says that when she ingested this substance everything was easier, the relationship with clients, meeting the schedule without difficulties (she was never sleepy), her relationship with friends, although her personal fixation was to get pregnant, she needed to have a child in the short term (she repeated this several times).

The truth is that she was very straightforward, very plain-spoken and with a strong, energetic tone of voice. She was young, by my estimates not even 25.

Some patient sheets, when they don't have a serious diagnosis, show the date of birth, but the truth is that I never look at it, it doesn't interest me at all. In my imagination, a session that was going to be dynamic and engaging was coming to my mind.

And I had in mind a *practice point* from the APS:

- In a multidisciplinary team, clinicians will maintain an appropriate pace of speech, pauses and turn-taking by all parties to facilitate quality and accurate delivery of messages to the patient.

However, as theory is one thing and practice is another, it is not always easy to find a suitable reality to manage and to direct towards APS counselling. It must be assumed that this can be achieved through constructive dialogue or mutual partnership.

The DT seemed a bit overwhelmed by the story, she even had to look at her PC in front of us, which was really extasis and information about it. It should be noted that this was an initial appointment, no diagnosis of a drug problem had been previously made.

The junior DT's, especially at the GP, were using google with total disregard. It was all there. There was the truth. The beginning and the end of the universe. The DT was checking extasis data.

Initially, she had asked me to repeat the translation three times, although the word in the source language of the PA hardly changes, it was clear that it had taken her by surprise, she didn't know what extasis was. With her youth, I guess she had never had such a case before.

At first, the DT was hesitant in her questions, asking about the effects that PA-06 noticed when taking the substance mentioned and if she took other drugs, and if she drank alcohol.

The answer was yes, she took some cocaine (she said she smoked), other pills (few) that she didn't know what they were, she simply swallowed them (those given to her by friends) and that was it, a lot of alcohol, but only beer at the end of the work (during the working hours she didn't drink alcohol, only sofdrinks).

The DT took a passive, stand-by attitude, the PA-06 kept on talking, it was difficult for me to follow her line of argument and I asked her to calm down a bit in order to carry out the translation in a well-coordinated way.

It was apparent that the DT assumed that her excessively intemperate state of mind was due to the fact that the PA had come to the consultation under the effects of some substance.

She barely listened, she talked and talked with her eyes fixed on a wall, she didn't even look at us.

The DT was still calm, and she had decided to turn her PC screen towards us, it was as if we were in the living room having coffee. Or maybe her tactic was the best, I don't know, the number of focuses that the PA-06 offered were too many to estimate and follow up in a coordinated way. As for me, the translation was still going on, and my effort was being very substantial.

And another APS *practice point* came to mind:

- Clinicians should pause and avoid overlapping speech, speaking at a reasonable speed, matching the interpreter in their translation.

DT: Don't worry, everything will be fine.

PA-06 touched both knees with both hands and leaned forward, as if trying to understand the meaning of those words and promptly applied to the DT for pills.

DT: Don't worry, we're going to help you, it's going to be fine.

The PA-06 kept touching her knees, it was like she was trying to pull down her skirt, she had it at the level of her knees and being seated it was totally out of reach, but she was trying to stretch the fabric tightly, you could feel the tension in her hands.

Little by little I was able to understand the tactics of the DT. I had not noticed but it was evident that there was a visible margin of aggressiveness in the approach of the PA-06, hence, the responses of the DT so far as if she was looking for a moment of relaxation to start acting. It seemed to me that she knew what she was after and I felt at ease. The session was already becoming long, and verbally unstoppable. And she succeeded, little by little PA-06 was relaxing and speaking more calmly. Now the DT had begun to manage the session. The meeting was scheduled for 45 minutes and we had already been there for more than an hour. I was starting to get tired but of course it was just my own fantasy, I had not finished the session yet.

The DT dealt with the matter strongly, first of all as is logical and, given that it was a first consultation, needed a definite breakdown, to which the PA-06 reacted with acceptance. Everything was on hold for a second follow-up session. She would receive the msn on her mobile with the date and time of the appointment.

When I was leaving the PA-06 invited me for a drink. I told her I couldn't because I was busy with family matters. She told me that she was in agreement with what the DT said, but that she had to take pills and she had only prescribed Paracetamol (I don't know if this is true because I didn't have the chance to see the prescription).

She told me that she was going to take initiative, that she wanted to live in *Middle*, that the night was overtaking her, that she didn't like her job and many other things. I tried to remind her that the session was over, that if she needed my help as a translator she could contact me at the agency, but that I had no clue about meds or counselling.

******

PA-58.

PA-58 was devastated because she had broken up with her boyfriend. They had taken a trip weeks ago, a trip to Bharat that she had asked her partner for as a gift. They had visited that city, PA-58 was thrilled and excited to make the trip that for her was a dream, a real fairy tale.

Now, weeks later, since they had returned to Middle, everything had completely changed. Her boyfriend had moved out on her (they had been living together until then). She was very anxious, heartbroken and sad.

The PA continued with her performance. In fact, it was as if she had prepared it, as if she had memorised her story before she came. I say this because he would lean back in his chair, look at the DT, and start talking consecutively, only stopping to let me translate, but he would look at me and straight away, after my translation, he would resume again without pause.

PA-58 would talk and talk, like IT translating, and the DT would listen. I came to think if the DT was really listening, he didn't say anything, he seemed to be somewhere else. She was even looking at her mobile phone messages while PA-58 was still going around Bharat.

The talk was really a monologue and the story seemed to be straight out of a tourist brochure of "things to do in Bharat" or "places to visit in Bharat". He mentioned various places in the city, the hotel where they had stayed, the journeys they had made and much more. Everything was fantastic, wonderful, unforgettable, a dream holiday.

The DT was still on her mobile, the PA-58 was looking at me and waiting for the translation. Of a certainty it was a somewhat atypical session, it was out of the norm. It was like a friendly discussion over a cup of tea and chocolate biscuits. There lacked pictures of Bharat on the table and shots of the couple riding camels.

The only thing is, don't ask me why or why not, but it was one of the few occasions, when attending this kinda sessions, that I had the personal glimpse that most of the things that the PA-58 told, were not true, that she was inventing many of the scenes, as if she was a compulsive liar or something, I don't know, I'm probably wrong, it was just an instant impression.

Suddenly the DT asked: Are you pregnant?.

The problem was that she was devastated, absolutely depressed because, once they had returned from Bharat, her partner had left her, they had broken up, he had moved out of the flat they shared. They were no longer together.

Now, several weeks later, she was seeking psychological help, because she didn't even step out of the house, she was extremely depressed and yes, according to the tests she had done, she was pregnant, which made her negative-depressed state even worse.

PA-58: I want to get out of this. I want to be alive again. I feel very weak. Why did it have to happen?. Everything was going so well?. Now far from my country, alone, what am I going to do?.

The DT asked her to calm down. She asked her to stay in control, she was going to help her, after all, the pregnancy should be seen as something posssitive.

PA-58: Having a child doesn't upset me, but I'm frustrated that his father won't be with us.

DT: If he didn't want to be a father, that's really his problem. Don't you have any relatives who can help you?.

PA-58: My mother was visiting Middle a year ago, but she's back in our country. I don't know, that might be the same thing I have to do, to leave this country, I don't know.

DT: For the moment, you have to calm that anxiety. Follow up on your pregnancy in its early stages and take care of your health.

PA-58: Yes, but at home I can't stop crying, I don't feel strong enough.

The conversation was extensive, with several comments from the DT, advice and mentions of helpful medication, which gradually managed to calm the patient down. We said goodbye. We did not see each other again.

*****

PA-12.

A private centre very close to the city centre. First visit of the PA-12. I had been waiting for him for more than half an hour when he was late. Sometimes, when the patient was more than half an hour late, the IT session was cancelled. In this case, we decided to wait.

The truth is that PA-12 looked like one of those homeless people on the street, smelled pretty bad and dressed as if she had been sleeping on the street for weeks. As far as I could make out, this was his first visit to this Centre.

His main problem was that, according to him, he had been sleeping no more than 3-4 hours a day, or even less, for several weeks, which had worsened his personal life considerably and, by the way, he had lost his job some time ago. The thing is that he was pretending to be one of those people who liked to break the social rules.

As in most of these cases, the psychologist, although she already had the patient's records (supposedly from the NHS), wanted to hear PA-12's own side of the story. It didn't take long for him to confess that he had been a permanent cocaine addict for quite a long period of time. He told us, and asked me to translate, how his world had shrunk, and how he felt a brutal depression that prevented him from sleeping, among other complaints. He spoke and expressed himself in a firm, very forceful way, conveying veracity in everything he said. The psychologist waited for a translation, took notes and continued with her list of pre-established questions.

The session was highly intriguing, PA-12, despite his ailments, had a peculiar sense of humour and told of his regular habit of taking cocaine only to suddenly stop, his lack of sleep, his financial problems, and how his wife had left him.

Certainly, his addiction seemingly had struck his life head on, or at least that's what he told us. He was now facing abstinence.

DT: One of the results of social influence is the development of social norms. Ways of thinking, feeling or behaving that are shared by group members and perceived by them as appropriate. Norms include customs, traditions, standards and rules, as well as the general values of the group.

Your Middle's new values are being handled in the wrong way. You need to get to grips with these new norms, at least accept them for the time you are here, especially as you say you want to live in the country for a long period of time.

DT: Through norms, we learn what people actually do and also what we should do (do to others what you would like them to do to you) and what we should not do. It might be a case of maladjustment to the new environment in your new country. We need to work on that.

Today I need a bit of relaxation, I need the session to have some jazz music in the background. My mind wanders for a few seconds of the session (the ones the DT is using for personal check-ups) and I imagine the PA-12 with a guitar in his hand, wearing a Hawaiian shirt and a daikiri on the table, the DT smoking menthol cigarettes and me translating from a deckchair, but it's all a fiction, the DT comes back and there's nothing like that.

The DT made a few parentheses to include theoretical points:

Withdrawal syndrome is one of the risks of cocaine use. It can occur when a person uses cocaine repeatedly over a period of time and then stops or cuts down abruptly. Cocaine withdrawal can include physical and psychological symptoms.

It is a sign of dependence, where the body becomes dependent on a drug to function. When a person stops taking the drug or reduces the quantity of cocaine taken, they may experience withdrawal symptoms as the body adjusts to not having the drug.

Cocaine withdrawal syndrome can involve a number of uncomfortable physical and psychological/behavioural symptoms. The most prevalent signs include:

- Deeply dysphoric mood. Depression (which may include suicidal thoughts).
- Anxiety. Irritability. fatigue sluggish mental or physical energy slowness of movement.
- persistent cravings for drugs difficulty sleeping or oversleeping.
- vivid dreams or nightmares difficulty concentrating memory problems.

DT: you do have to be equipped to face these challenges. Let's work on it together.

Strangely, PA-12 diverted the conversation and began to make religious references. He said that Jesus Christ was his support and that with his help, his life would get easier, that he had a New Testament in his dorm room to consult. Yes, the help of Jesus, he will help me get through this. He mentioned another book (he didn't say the title), which spoke of Jesus' death, how he had suffered and how his journey to the Cross and his last words would help the helpless. He said that he was just another disciple and that he was waiting for salvation.

The psychologist, on the edge of these religious notes, did not hesitate to ask: have you had thoughts of suicide?. PA-12 leaned back in his chair, looked at the psychologist and said: Yes, I do (silence).

PA-12 argued that he needed a communicative therapy, he felt that when he talked to an expert he was relieved and, when he got home, he could better tackle his everyday problems (he had been living with her mother since his wife left him).

On the other hand, he was afraid, he didn't want to consume again, but it was very painful for him to make that choice. When he didn't take, everything went black. The psychologist took notes and listened. There was no comment on it.

The DT offers a twist to the session. Raises comments on cultural differences, asks questions to PA-12, if he already had these addictive consumption problems when he was in his country, before coming to the Middle.

DT: It is important to be aware of cultures and cultural differences, at least partly because more and more people from different cultural backgrounds are coming into contact with each other as a result of increased travel and immigration.

The DT went into action again with assertive questions:

DT: Do you feel oppressed in this society?. Do you see yourself as a victim?. Do you feel marginalised?.

PA-12: I don't know, I like the food here. Sometimes, I spend several days without eating almost anything. Sweets or chocolates are my food for days.

DT: But, your environment. Do you notice hostility?. Do you feel the contrast with your country of origin?. Do you feel you are affected by the new life habits?.

PA-12: I don't know, I like living here. It was my wife's idea to come here.

The answers of the PA-12 did not keep the DT satisfied, who fixed her gaze on me and proposed to the PA-12 to take a psychological test, with three answers to each question, and he had to choose one of the three (he had to mark one of the three with a pen in the corresponding box after the translation).

The test was about five pages long, so you were advised to answer quickly and not to think too much. We stood at the next table answering these questions.

Essentially the questions showed the relevance of the pressures of consent in social groups and how people in power could create dependability, even to the point of leading people to cause serious harm to others.

The centre we were in was situated in a comfortable area, away from the noise and surrounded by greenery with several trees, the room had large glass windows, and we could see the rain falling in the background. It was a typical Middle winter afternoon.

I had no more sessions today, so I relaxed and assisted the PA-12 as much as I could. I wondered to myself, if the psychologist would be able to guess the image of the guitar and the deckchair, but I think her mind was far away, the distance between the IT and the contextualisation of the moment can also present its mental gaps.

The DT said that she was not going to treat it as an addiction issue in principle, since, as far as she understood, he was using cocaine but he controlled his use very effectively and it did not seem to be the source of the trouble. The question, however, went further. He thought we were dealing with a personality disorder.

PA-12 listened carefuly to my translation and said nothing, as if accepting whatever the DT chose to do in a constructive way. In this case, he kept looking as if waiting for some extra reasoning, which came at once from the DT, who began to relate a string of reasons for this disordered personality, trying to explain the connections with PA-12's case.

The PA had a big smile on his face and was constantly fingering his nose. He seemed amused, although I have no clue as to the reason.

13. Home-Visiting Process

PA-03.

Like other home visits, I had only the address of the building. It was a January morning, I remember it as it had been snowing for two days in Middle. The visit was about 5 kms away. I could make out a block of buildings, in the direction given. The one in the centre was the one in front of mine, quite ugly and I reckon about 12 storeys high. My stop was on the sixth floor. It was very cold.

As a rule, we were given a mobile phone number of the social worker, so that we could meet before entering the house. In this case, there were two people I was able to meet later at the front door of the building after some very direct text messages.

They were both very friendly, introduced themselves swiftly, were noticeably cold as well, and, without any further mediation, rang the doorbell. The door was opened by a woman in her 50s, maybe older, dressed in a breakfast cooking apron. She had shining eyes. The appointment was very early in the morning.

PA-03 and the DT spoke very warmly and we were invited into a living room, with a very comfortable sofa. It was actually surprising that in a building with a limited and ugly appearance, there were such spacious living quarters. There was plenty of space. A feeling of well-being.

The DT, as usual, went straight to the subject that brought us to this place. PA-88 was the object of the invitation. He was a teenager, the son of the woman who opened the door and was suffering from some disorders that I was not aware of at the time (I had not been informed so far).

The boy had a masturbation propensity and, according to the first explanatory sentences, he practised this activity in full view of everyone, i.e. he was fond of masturbating and did so anywhere in the house, especially in the bathroom, but with the door wide open.

DT: In children masturbation is triggered by their curiosity, as well as by hormonal impulses that are shifting naturally in their bodies. Many children also resort to masturbation to release tension, even without grasping the science behind it.

It should be added that he had two sisters, who lived in the same house and, as is to be expected, regarded his attitudes as totally inadmissible, although the DT made it clear that he had been previously been diagnosed (she did not say of what) and that he would now receive treatment and follow-up, because PA-03 was a friendly person who did not hurt anyone, and did not attack or harm anyone.

DT: Masturbation within a specific, safe and private space is actually quite healthy and does not cause long-term sexual health difficulties. It is not the masturbation that is harmful, but how we deal with it as parents when we "catch" them in the act.

His mother was outspoken in her comments, asking the DT for resolution, saying that there had already been many sessions and that she did not see any progress. The DT made it clear that this was a touchy subject and that it would require time.

The mother now said that it was a bad time in the family and that she did not wished to hamper the growth of her daughters with this issue and that she would sooner apply for an action such as a boarding school or something similar if her finances would allow it.

She said that her son was what she most loved, but that she didn't realise why he would do these things, why he would go to such levels of excess. The DT told her that he was acting unconsciously, that it was not a desired action, that most of these cases are psychological in nature, and that it was advisable to follow it up in order to find the best treatment for the family.

DT: However, as long as children masturbate in a public environment, it will have negative long-term effects. This will not help them understand the difference between a 'consensual touch' and a 'non-consensual touch' and prevent anyone from harming them sexually.

The DT sympathised with the mother's concern, because this was a case where the behaviour really signalled the need for medical or psychological treatment, not least because of the continuity of doing it in spaces where others could see him.

He no longer valued his own privacy. He was compulsively masturbating, although there were no signs so far that he was forcing other people around him to engage in sexual activity with him.

DT: While there are natural urges and behavior that are considered normal, there is also sexual behavior that can be worrying and needs psychological or medical assessment.

One of the daughters approached, everyone looked at her, she was wearing clothes as if she had just got out of the shower. She took something from the fridge on the side and without saying anything she left.

It was as if she was going to say something, but she preferred to keep quiet or that someone in her family had warned her not to step in. As far as I could see, there was no father, I mean, no one referred to a male father figure, nor was there anyone present.

As an IT, the talk, I must admit, was very fluent, and they were using a very common language that was easy to translate. I felt pretty comfy, because I was sitting on the edge of the sofa, far away from the mother, which was a good position to do my service.

The next translation was more complicated, because the DT was asking the mother to explain in detail some of those moments when her son was masturbating, let's say in front of everybody. According to her explanation, the aim was to pinpoint the reasons why he was jerking off.

She expressed that part of her concern was that she feared he was inciting her daughters to do it, she saw his attitude of doing it in public as the most worrying situation, as it would be natural that if he did it in private it would be almost within the bounds of what was normal for his age.

At least as a mother I had heard comments from other mothers that it was not a big surprise. But in public in front of family members and, time and again, it had its point of refusal that didn't need to be explained.

I was beginning to feel confused, because according to previous feedback, he had been diagnosed with a degree of backwardness. And there came one of those moments where translation is treacherous, in the early hours of the morning and with a mother who spoke bluntly.

Two days earlier, he had masturbated in the bathroom, at about 3pm, just when one of her sisters was having a visit from two friends. It had been very embarrassing for everyone. The reactions had been astonished, and the mother acknowledged that her concern was growing. The sister acknowledged that she was hardly going to invite her friends to her house.

The details, including all sorts of facts, were now not easy to translate, whether he had his member in his right hand but did not make gestures, whether he was fixed and static or not, whether he made any innuendo to those who passed in the hallway and saw him, etc.

The DT repeated questions, and the mother without much more, really strong in her stance, explained but without any aggressive looks, with no bad gestures, we were really becoming friends (there was a good feeling despite the topic being dealt with).

DT: Explain to your child that it is only natural to sometimes want to discover, and if they do, they should do it alone and in private, out of safety from the public danger of strangers. You can also redirect their attention by keeping their hands busy with something else instead.

DT: If the problem occurs regularly and doesn't die out, it is best to speak to their pediatrician and have them offer advice to your child as a health precaution during their next check-up.

At this point, already more than two hours into the talk, the DT reacted and did not want to go any further for the day. There was mention of a further meeting in about 20 days. I was grateful, I needed a break.

There were the appropriate farewells. At no time did we see PA-88. It was early, he was supposed to be sleeping. It had been a visit without the patient being present.

******

PA-02.

PA-02 lived in a very tall building, in an area of several comparable buildings. The surrounding environment itself was gelid. It was a case of Alheizmer. The woman was in bed, we had to wait for a nurse to move her to an adjoining room.

As far as I could tell, her condition was getting worse. It had been several years since she had been diagnosed with the disease, she was moving around in and around the house and was known to the relatives, however, since weeks ago everything had started to get worse. Now he no longer recognised any of his relatives. It was gradually becoming very unlikely that she could get out of bed. His level of general awareness had seriously deteriorated. In my previous knowledge, it was a matter of delimiting the current status of PA-02 and how her care and attention would be managed in the future.

One of the daughters had asked to be admitted to a private clinic, but one of the brothers did not agree.

Anyway, there were several issues and all of them very complex to be dealt with, although we would focus on knowing the level of consciousness of the PA-02. The DT would set up her tests and relevant variables and check with her superiors and/or family members.

PA-02 spoke almost without being asked, she reacted to our presence in a friendly way, like someone who is looking for a listener outside her usual environment. In any case, it was clear from the beginning that she was saying unconnected things, references that had no connection with us at all, and she spoke on impulse, then became silent for a long time, as if in thought.

It was also clear that the language was not the problem, she was able to communicate in the language that had been requested, in fact, she would stare at me and even try to grab my hand when she spoke. In fact, she looked like a frightened woman, bearing a strong inner anguish, it was difficult for me to keep my cool when she expressed herself.

To make ourselves understood, every time the DT asked her a question she listened and answered, but the answer was always unconnected, it had nothing to hand with what she had been asked.

Most of the answers started with a name, always referring to someone by name, although that person was neither a relative nor any of the people in the room. To put it in a frivolous way, but which helps to understand the context, it is as if someone asked me details about my private life and I responded with answers from a film I had seen weeks ago, nothing related.

If she referred to her name, it was in the third person. For example she would say:

PA: If she was there (her name), she was the one who did it, she moved the box.

If she was asked about a relative, she repeated the name several times, but nothing else:

DT: Have you seen Jaime (a brother)?.

PA-02: Yes, Jaime, Jaime, Jaime, Jaime (silence).

DT: Have you seen Mira (sister)?.

PA-02: Mira, Mira, Mira (silence).

DT: How old is Jaime?.

PA-02: (total silence).

DT: Have you had breakfast?.

PA-02: Breakfast, but what do you mean, breakfast (silence).

I have attended several cases of ALheizmer, but this was the most advanced without a doubt. The one in which the harmful and degenerative influence of Alzheimer's on the patient was most clearly visible.

Actually, it was very tough to keep the dialogue going, the people in the background by the window, quiet, but observing and with short references to the questions (only when they were about family matters). If one of them spoke for a long time, then PA-91 said absolutely nothing, no answer or anything else.

******

PA-53.

This is a controversial case because it could not be carried out. It was a private nursing home in the Middle area. The surrounding streets, in the centre of town, were bustling with passers-by. It was lunchtime on a November morning in the middle of winter. There was a gentle, yet biting wind.

The residence was close by, it was easy to spot. It was the first time I had visited this centre. The outer door was locked, I had to knock and to identify myself, to be allowed entry to the interior. The atmosphere inside was really cosy, the heating was working well and according to the needs.

I was sitting on a sofa waiting for someone to assist me. An older lady came up to me, slim and with a leisurely gait. She had a smile on her lips, checked my badge and the PA-53 details and, certifying that everything was in order, she had written down in a notebook at the entrance the attendance of an IT, which was me, and she had also marked very carefully the name of the PA-53.

DT: We have to go to room 422. Please follow me.

The lady inspired confidence, telling me the rough picture of the patient's condition, who had already been in the hospice for quite some time. According to what she said, she had worsened in the last few weeks, hence the reason for this meeting with the IT, because she was a foreigner, spoke little English and had lost her auditory capacity.

Their state of health was deteriorating, they were in that critical phase, where it was imperative to verify the person's real ability to fend for themselves. I had seen such cases before, so I was not taken by surprise. She also reported to me that we would have to wait for two other people, a social worker who had attended her previously and another person who she told me was a specialist, although she did not tell me what position she held.

The residence was spacious, we were still walking all the time on the ground floor. I could see several rooms at the back, one of them had the number 422 on the door: target point.

The door was completely open, the room was very spacious, much more than others I had seen before in this type of residences, it reflected a warm and comfy atmosphere with all kinds of accessories, including some armchairs, a sofa and others. At the back, near the window, was the bed. The PA-53 was on the couch, something that was pointed out to me right away.

With her was a young girl, less than 30 years old, I thought she was a relative, or a daughter, but no, I was told she was a nurse. She seemed completely unaware of our presence.

The PA-53 was sitting quietly without much fuss, she gave the appearance of a well cared for old lady, she was even wearing a light blue dungarees with a red duck pattern. It was as if she had been well arranged for this meeting. The room smelled very nice, more like a high-class sauna than a room in an old people's home.

The nurse was also very well dressed, she was not wearing a medical gown, which is why I did not initially associate her as such. She was wearing beige trousers and a soft green blouse, which made her look like a shop assistant from the Primark chain.

When she saw me, she mumbled something like: yes, yes, I know, a translator, yes of course, I've seen others before, yes I know, the one who translates.

The way she had been expressing herself seemingly uncharacteristically, and it made me suspicious, there was something weird about her, or at least that was my first impression, and sadly, I wasn't wrong. She was going to be the guest star of this meeting.

As for me, I was still standing near the door, I was waiting for the arrival of the DT and, while I never agreed on these visits to sit down or go near the PA-53, it didn't take long for them to arrived. They shook my hand and gave me a quick overview of the situation and how the matter was going to be handled. They saw the nurse and asked her who she was.

She replied, but not in a friendly manner. The staff immediately realised her manner and told her that they understood that she was the nurse, but that she would have time to do her job later, she would have to leave the room now because they had questions to ask PA-53 and they needed to know if she was capable of answering or what her physical and mental state was.

That's what they all were there for. While they were saying these lines, the lady who had greeted me in the lobby was still standing next to me. She figured it was time to leave, turned to the outside and pulled the door gently without closing it all the way, leaving it half-open.

We all expected the nurse to do the same, following the previous guidelines, but no, with a much louder tone of voice she said, that she was not moving from there. Oddly, she spoke in response to what the attendants said but fixed her eyes on me.

Then, he continued saying, always looking at me: yes, yes of course, the translator, I know, I know what that's all about.

His tone sounded quite unpleasant, there was a joke of irony or sarcasm or criticism towards me, as a translator, that none of the people present had understood. As I said, I had never been to this clinic before and I didn't know this young woman at all.

The other assistant, the specialist (I was not told in which field), approached her and, in a very gentle and calm tone, told her that he could not be present, that it would just be about 30-40 minutes, but that only the IT could be present, because of the language barrier, but that they needed the PA-53 to be alone.

He also mentioned that this was a usual procedure in these cases, of which the management of the clinic had been notified beforehand, and that it was not a matter of chance, but that there were rules of the process. We all had to adapt to a protocol.

The young woman replied:

- Not at all. I'm not going to leave her alone with one of those foreign translators and two blacks.

She said this in an aggressive tone and in a loud voice. I was shocked. The two assistants were black, yes they were, presumably from an African country living in Middle. There were many African social workers-assistants with dual nationality, I had already met others, people from Africa, now married and living with dual nationality in Middle.

Needless to say, there were moments of pause and silence. For my part, nothing to say, for the moment the PA-53 had not spoken, so the conversation between the others was in English, there was no need for any translation.

The main social worker (I remember one was a woman), was apparently oblivious to the offensive comment she had just heard and with a soft smile said:

- I am very sorry that you have that image of us. We are professionals working for years on these cases and we have to get on with our duties. We would appreciate it if you would leave the room.

The young woman kept looking at me. I don't know why, they were responding to her but she was looking at me, it was unusual. The situation was tense, with no apparent excuse, hard to comprehend.

The young woman replied:

- No way. I will not leave you alone.

They looked at each other, the two assistants, and together they went to the window, as if turning their backs to the young woman. They whispered things to each other, without us being able to hear them.

They retraced their steps. They said that this was highly irregular and that they didn't have any idea of their motives. In any case, in order to avoid tight tension, it was already late today, but first thing tomorrow morning they would talk to the management of the clinic to resolve the unpleasant circumstance.

They were going to cancel the meeting, but they also made it clear to her that they were holding her fully to blame for the delay of the meeting, for its implications and for having to call in another interpreter again. The girl said nothing.

She sat down on the sofa and picked up her mobile phone to text. To tell the truth, no one in the room was able to grasp what was happening to her, nor did we understand who she was, if she was a real nurse.

In view of the complex situation, and given that they decided to announce the cancellation, I said that I was leaving, and that they knew where to contact if they needed a translator again. The representative was very cordial and thanked me for my attendance. She signed my visit form herself. I nodded and left.

The exit door could be opened from the inside with the inside release button, so I didn't have to wait for help. I left, somewhat disgruntled but feeling some relief. The entire scenario was very intriguing and, in these cases, cancellation was the best thing to do.

******

PA-64.

PA-64 had been involved in a traffic accident which had resulted in total quadriplegia (complete cervical spinal cord injury). He will have to struggle for the rest of his life, although it was hardly imaginable, but he could consider himself lucky to be alive (given the enormity of the accident).

From the evidence his wife gave me of the accident, PA-64 was not at the fault of the accident. He was simply in an area of the road waiting for his turn to pass on the left hand side of the road, on a motorbike, when a speeding car invaded his lane, taking him with it. The crash was devastating, his wife told me, because the speed of the car was much higher than the speed allowed in an urban area.

He had been in hospital for a long time, and now he was scheduled to undergo a consultation to check his physical progress, follow-up and also because he had to update his situation in the residence that had been granted to him. He was possibly going to be sent to another one with similar criteria but better conditioned. Final confirmation was pending.

What was most surprising about this man (accompanied at all times by his wife) was that, apart from the fact that he was in a wheelchair, he had a very flattering appearance, If you could only see his upper body, the upper part of his body, in a picture, it would be absolutely impossible to guess his real state of health. He looked like a strong person and outwardly, including his face, he had no marks from the accident.

He obviously had many health problems as a result of the accident, not only mobility problems, but his intellect was fully intact. He spoke very fluently, knew what he wanted and knew how to listen to the DT's explanations.

They lived in a very quiet and comfortable area, in private ground floor housing, which had been granted to him as an aid to his disability. The house was very well equipped and with details oriented to his dysfunction.

Now in his home the first thing he would have to learn was to find his personal mobility options, i.e. to learn to do basic things for himself, mostly bed mobility and even some more major steps.

The DT taught him a basic but very powerful technique, with the use of a small board, to be able to step out of the bed into his wheelchair without the help of anyone else, on his own. It was practised several times, PA-64 was very excited, he had his wife but the idea of doing it by himself filled his eyes with joy.

We went to the toilet, a vital point in this training session. Other techniques were applied by the therapist so that PA-64 practised options of using the most basic items in the washbasin.

He had been struggling with this, he still needed a lot of practice, but the DT was giving him advice on how to move forward with the help of his wife, looking for the high point of potential independence in the future. The DT for his part would make regular visits to help him weeks later.

Another request he made was to have his wheelchair changed, as it was a bit too small for him. Almost all the cases I saw with patients in wheelchairs asked for their wheelchair to be changed (it was very common), although the requests took a long time. It should not be forgotten that this was an accessory that was provided free of charge to the patient at that time.

The woman remained in the background, leaving him to make requests and comments. She expressed herself very precisely, her ideas were clear when it came to fighting against the handicap in a personal and almost professional way, seeking the support of the specialist, and that is why she was so forceful.

The dialogues were clear, precise and easy to translate. All the terminology used was quite common and quite readily identifiable from other cases I had had and from the context in which we were moving.

There was a final time in the kitchen. His recent medical tests were checked. His physical evolution according to them was satisfactory, there had been improvements within the seriousness of the case.

*****

PA-25.

The patient had requested a home consultation because he had a knee problem, it was temporary and he could not move around properly. However, his consultation was about something else. Today a DT visited and provided him with information about his condition. She also made a note of an option to go for further hospital treatment, once his knee was fixed.

He was reported urinary problems to the DT, such as a weak flow when he urinates, a feeling that his bladder has not emptied properly, difficulty starting to urinate and dribbling urine after finish urinating.

DT considered that these symptoms can also be caused by different things, such as cold weather, anxiety, other health problems, lifestyle factors and some medicines. In either way, in this case, it would be a matter of defining whether the PA-25 is facing prostate enlargement (that was the approach of the previous consultation).

PA: Actually, I'm quite worried. At the last visit to the hospital, I was told that my prostate had almost certainly increased in size, that I had an enlarged prostate. Can I cope with it with medication?.

DT: We still don't really know all the things that cause the prostate to grow. but we do know about two factors that can increase your risk of having an enlarged prostate.

It's supposed DT must to verify the balance of hormones (oestrogen and testosterone(in his body changes. This may cause his prostate to grown. the risk increases also as getting older.

Next questions to the PA-25 where focus, about family connections, he could be more at risk od developing it if his father or brother has one. DT asked also about diabetes and daily habits as regular exercise.

PA-25: Am I more likely to get prostate cancer if I have an enlarged prostate?.

DT: No, having and enlarged prostate does not increase your risk of getting prostate cancer. The two problems usually begin in different parts of the prostate. But men can have an enlarged prostate and prostate cancer at the same time.

PA-25: How might an enlarged prostate affect my life?.

DT: Having an enlarged prostate affects men in different ways. Some men can manage symptoms and don't need treatment. Other men find they need to stay near a toilet. this can make it difficult to work, drive, be outdoors and attend social events. If you need the toilet a lot during the night, this can affect your sleep and make you feel more tired during the day.

Some men with an enlarged prostate find their symptoms improve over time without treatment. But for most, the symptoms will stay the same or slowly start to cause more problems over time unless they have treatment.

DT suggest ways to help manage his symptoms, and will arrange for him to see a hospital specialist. the specialist may do other tests, such as a urine flow test and and ultrasound scan. Depending on the results, he may have further tests at the hospital, such as a bladder pressure test, a flexible cystoscopy and a pad test.

PA-25: What are my treatment options?.

DT: there are three main types of treatment for an enlarged prostate:

- lifestyle changes.

- medicines.

- surgery.

If test show you have an enlarged prostate, we will look at your test results and medical history to see which treatments might be suitable. You need to visit the hospital as soon as possible. Anyway, there are simple changes you can make to your lifestyle that might help your symptoms:

- drink less alcohol, caffeine, artificial sweeteners and fizzy drinks.

- drink less in the evening.

- eat more fruit and fibre.

- check your medicines.

- empty your bladder before leaving the house.

- keep a healthy weight.

- exercise regularly.

- urethral massage.

DT: For the moment we will wait for the results and then we will have another appointment.

******

PA- 105.

The morning was an aggressive winter, it was raining heavily, it was wet and cold. It was almost 11am and I was waiting for the DT to arrive. Two text messages to be sure about the meeting and little else. We entered the apartment building just 5 minutes before the appointment. The DT gave me information about the case. It seemed to be a case of conflict. In principle, before going to the flat, we would have to check at the service desk that our patient had paid his rent.

They had got married a few months earlier and, according to her, they suspected that it was a marriage arranged by the young man to take advantage of the older woman.

It seems that the young man, given PA-105's wheelchair situation, took over her monthly allowance and was always at home in the flat rented by the lady, not working or looking for work, i.e. taking advantage of her.

On the other hand, he had not paid the rent for several months, only because he was the one who managed the payments, the lady had never stopped paying when she lived alone. Moreover, it was incomprehensible not to pay, as she had a flat with a very low rent, which was very affordable compared to her income.

This issue got on the DT's nerves, as he thought it was an absolute disgrace that she had a very low rent and was not paying. Customer Services confirmed that no one had paid the rent for her flat and that it was several months in arrears.

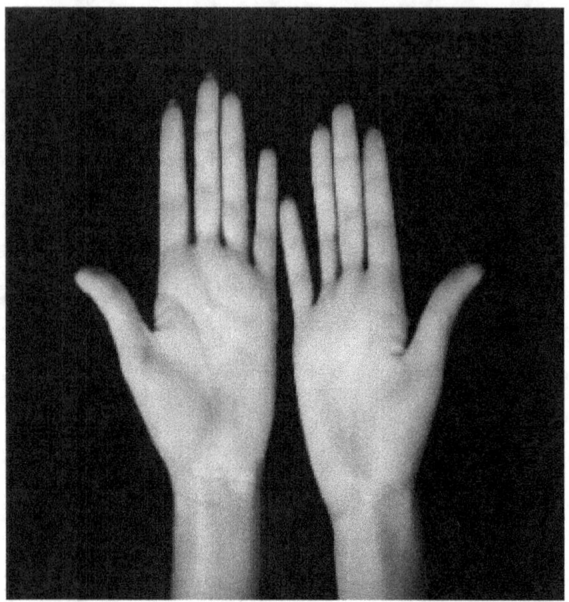

Finally, we took the lift to her flat. They were both waiting for the visit. The lady was in a wheelchair and had several health problems, including some memory loss.

The DT started with a series of questions. They focused on her general health, whether she went out or never went out, what her routine was, whether she had any pain, what medication she took and how regularly she took it, and so on.

Gradually the questions moved on to the situation in the home and the relationship. It must be said that at this point the questions were very direct, she just asked and asked to assess the husband's contribution at home, his behaviour, how he managed his salary, what things he did or didn't do.

The truth is that the wife's answers, although they were slow and sometimes she had to translate twice for her to understand the meaning, were always neutral, I mean in her evaluations of her husband she never said anything negative, although it has to be taken into account that the husband was present and looking at her.

The husband tried to add a personal comment between the questions. When it came to this part of the questionnaire, as soon as he realised that they were all evaluating him and his behaviour, he showed first displeasure and then total disgust.

He said that he did not understand why these questions were being asked, let alone in his presence, and that it was really offensive. The DT made no changes but simply replied directly that he should keep quiet while his wife answered the questions as they were directed at her as the PA.

The husband could not bear the answer, showed his disagreement and went into the kitchen. There was a wall between them, but the kitchen was close by and he left the door open, so he could obviously hear the conversation without any problem.

It was time for the two most controversial questions. First, why the rent had not been paid. This question was asked aloud, indirectly by the DT to her husband, somewhat ironically as she had just told him not to interfere.

The husband took the hint perfectly and came to us very excited. He said that the rent would be paid next week, that it was no big deal, that there were only a few arrears.

The DT immediately reminded him that the problem had only arisen because he was the one handling the income from the house. This statement made the husband, who was now pacing back and forth from the kitchen under the gaze of his wife, even more furious.

He promised that he would pay the rent next week, that he would pay all the arrears. In a bad mood and from the kitchen, from a distance, but that's what he said. The DT made a dead end, a moment of silence. Immediately the second contradictory question. Apparently the lady had been using the food delivery service for some time, by which I mean the service run by the DT. There was a kind of catering service for sick people with mobility problems, and she was offered the opportunity to order food from the catalogue they had.

It appeared that the lady had been using it Monday to Friday for the lunch menu, which she had been doing on a regular basis. Now the DT had noticed that the husband had partially cancelled this service, leaving only one home delivery of food for Friday of each week.

The DT, not understanding why he had almost completely cancelled these food deliveries, asked for an explanation, but first asked the PA-105 whether she was aware of this situation and whether she had made the decision together with her husband, or whether her husband alone was partly responsible for this decision.

Of course, the DT was very direct and implied that it was her husband's decision alone and attacked him as a manipulator, although she did not use that word, but her detours were very direct and the meaning of her words was very clear.

The husband, as expected, feeling attacked, came back to us from the kitchen and this time addressed his wife directly, asking her to be the one to answer so that we could see that he was not guilty.

PA-105, watching her husband's comings and goings and listening to the DT's assessments, did not know what to say at first. After some silence, she said that he was cooking and that there was no shortage of food, that there was always something to eat.

It should be remembered that PA-105 was also beginning to have some memory problems, which in principle should be assessed in his development. Sometimes he did not understand the questions well, he did not understand the meaning and of course he always took a long time to answer.

She didn't say much more about the food, she remained silent, now with her head down, as if she was thinking, or as if she didn't care about the situation.

The husband took action, opened the fridge and started taking things out and putting them on the kitchen table. He had told us to go into the kitchen, which was only a few steps away. She listened to the DT and could see several plates of food in the fridge.

The man said that he was a good cook and that he always prepared something for the next day in the evening. He didn't understand her assessment because they didn't need to order out when they had food at home. Besides, he said, his wife had never complained.

Not much was said by the DT, who looked at the food shown to her and kept a silence of relative approval, because her gestures said otherwise. The PA-105 was now completely silent, asked if she agreed, and as soon as she answered, she just raised her arm and pointed at her husband, as if to tell us to ask him.

She clearly gave the impression that she was tired. The DT also noticed this and said that that was enough for today. She would arrange another visit. In the meantime, I hoped that the rent payment would be real and that the food situation would be assessed in terms of the outcome of the PA's food. The husband made a gesture towards me as if he did not understand what I was saying.

The husband replied that if it took too long to make another appointment, they might not be there because, given the situation, he was seriously considering going back to his home country and taking his wife with him.

The DT replied that in the state the PA was in, travelling might not be the best idea. The husband replied that he had thought about it, but that she looked quite well and he was sure she could cope with the trip and that she would thank him for it afterwards.

The DT nodded her head in denial, but without saying anything in particular. She did not seem surprised by this announcement of a possible trip.

Although the tension was present for most of the visit, we said goodbye and there was a cordial farewell. However, in the corridor at the entrance to the lift and before the husband closed the door to the flat, she reminded him once again that he had to pay the rent. The man turned his head to the side and immediately closed the door with considerable force.

*****

PA- 81.

The visit was in the middle of the morning, I had to be home by 11am. I arrived half an hour early and sat in a cafe across the street waiting for the DT. It was raining heavily, it really was a rainy morning.

The DT rang the doorbell, it was a ground floor flat, typical of the houses in this town, with the front door under the stairs leading up to the main building. A young woman answered the door. She asked us who we were and went to call her mother. The mother was PA-81. First she said that she had not received any notice that the DT would be visiting her today.

Anyway, she invited us in. From the first moment I noticed that she was only talking to the DT, she didn't even look at me.

The house looked better inside than it did on the outside. It was spacious and had a very large light source from the ceiling in the middle of the main room. It was not the DT's first visit, I had been here before, but it was the first time for me.

With PA-81 was her 16 year old daughter and another 14 year old son who was apparently sleeping in the room, we could not see him. She had another son, aged 18, but he had gone out. After the introductions, we moved on to the case in question.

It was a case of domestic violence. The PA had called the police and reported her partner several times for assault. The DT had helped her with this problem with psychological support and now she was also looking for subsidies or grants because she could not afford to pay the rent.

The partner was not with her, i.e. he had left the house, but appeared on rare occasions to, according to the PA-81, threaten her and try to enter the house to assault her. She was able to show her upper neck and back where there were several marks which she said had been made a few days earlier when her boyfriend had visited her and then beaten her.

This was a difficult case to follow up. Firstly, because according to the DT, and by her own admission, she had been in another country years ago and had had to leave for the same reason, i.e. the partner who had assaulted her (he was not the same man as now). This question and the way the facts were presented led the DT to doubt the veracity of the facts.

Let's not forget that many migrant couples, when they are in financial difficulties or when it is difficult to obtain visas, use domestic violence as a weapon to get their wives and children to obtain legal documents in the country as a protective measure.

There are many cases where gender-based violence does not exist, but is invented to achieve their goals of staying in the country. In other cases, they go as far as self-harm, or the husband actually beats them, but always by mutual agreement, it is something that is prepared in order to make complaints and get documents later.

As far as I could tell, the DT had taken her time to assess the situation very well. Now she had decided to help the PA. She was processing her application for Housing Benefit and other benefits as she had two minor children. At the moment I had to wait and unfortunately the PA-81 had received a notice to leave because she had not paid.

My job was difficult, the PA only wanted to talk to the DT, I think because she was a woman. It was very obvious that she was rejecting me because I was a man. Maybe she could not distinguish between one person and another, maybe she was one of those cases who believes that if a man beats her, all men are murderers.

She was very unpleasant, spoke very fast and ignored my translation, which was necessary because the one who spoke (a little) English was the daughter and, as a minor, she was not supposed to intervene, but the mother did not care. The meeting was difficult.

The PA-81 became more and more aggressive and she began to blame the DT, saying that many visits had been made to her home but she didn't see any results. She didn't understand why they didn't help her, she was a victim and she had children, she needed help.

The decor of the room we were in was Arabic. There were small sofas, coloured fabrics on the walls, lots of cushions even on the floor, spotlights on the sides with no light, a red carpet and curtains on the sides giving access to the next room. The PA was drinking tea, although she was not offering the DT. Only she drank tea, not her daughter.

She had a long wooden spoon in her hand all the time, the kind you use in cooking when you have to stir large quantities of food. She would put the spoon down while drinking tea, but then pick it up again and hold it in her right hand.

It reminded me of the batons used by policemen or the sticks used by some security guards, as if to mark a distance or to protect themselves in case of attack. The PA took the same stance with the long spoon.

On the other hand, it made no sense for him to have it, there was no reason for it, it was not a valid tool for any activity at that time. I was very surprised that the DT didn't ask him why he was holding that spoon. It was very long and had a steel-coated handle.

She lifted her shirt again and showed me the marks on his back. She said it hurt and he needed help. How was he going to pay the rent, she said. The situation was critical, she had received several payment notices and this was the last one, she would have to leave the house, where would she go, she said.

The DT offered him various documents to sign, applications for assistance and others. It took some time to process, but the DT offered to speed up the process in any way he could.

The PA signed the documents but added that she was fed up with these home visits and did not see the point. She added that she did not like the presence of a male interpreter either. She said that she would like us to leave as soon as possible and not bother her any more.

PA-92.

PA-92 was a young woman under 30, looked worried and was wearing jeans with a black jumper and a jacket to withstand the winter cold. I could see her waiting for my arrival. It was early in the morning, there were no other patients so I went straight to ask her if she was expecting IT.

It was a hospital in Middle. It was one of the few times I made appointments on a Saturday and early in the morning, which might be why there was no one there. I asked at the counter and a friendly young lady gave me the number of the DT's office, he was inside, she said, waiting for all of you.

PA-92 started by saying that she had a sexual problem, her vagina was swollen and very painful. The DT reacted quickly and said that this should be examined. He said that he was a man and that he had better assign a nurse to check her as a woman.

The nursing service was on the same floor and she would only have to change rooms and then come back. The young woman nodded. In the meantime, she was willing to share more details with the DT.

The DT asked her, before the nurse's examination, if she thought it might be a sexual infection. She said that she was married and only had sexual relations with her husband. She clarified that it was the first time she had had something of this nature.

The DT inquired her if she had noticed anything about her husband, or if he had told her about any similar symptoms. He said yes, that he, too, had severe itching, a reddish appearance, discomfort when urinating and the discharge of a whitish pus, but that he had not been willing to come to the clinic. He thought it was nothing to be serious.

The DT replied that they were going to wait for a check-up, but that what he had just told him confirmed his suspicions of a sexually transmitted disease, as his husband's symptoms were the usual ones for this type of transmitted disease.

The nurse knocked on the door, said she was available, that I could go with her. I stood in the hallway waiting for her to come back from the check-up, and we went back inside. While the DT, had a short chat with the nurse, took some notes and told the PA-92 that they could also take a urine test (urinalysis).

However, pending the results of her urine test, he was going to prescribe treatment, as he found her prognosis to be very apparent. He advised her to ask her husband to come in for a urine test, he was going to prescribe her separate medication anyway, he too would have to take it if the problem remained unresolved. This medication would help to stop the discharge and the itching.

He made it clear to her that sexually transmitted diseases have to be treated for both partners, as they are a stable couple, and if she takes the medication and her husband does not, once they have sexual relations, the infection problems will return.

He gave her separate prescriptions, making it clear which meds were for her and which were for the husband, and the timing and dosage of how they were to be taken. She nodded with approval and some relief.

The DT concluded the session. He then asked her if she wanted to ask any questions before leaving. She asked just one last question:

- If I have sex only with my husband, how is it that I could have caught a sexually transmitted disease?.

The DT looked at both of us and said:

- It is presumably your husband who has transferred the disease. At times, it could be linked to a urine infection. The urinalysis will confirm this.

The young woman's expression was firm but with a certain degree of contradiction. She looked at the DT, and very politely thanked him for his attentions. We left the consulting room together.

On the way out, before we said goodbye, she told me that she was going to need a translator for a meeting with a family law attorney, and could I help her as an interpreter. I told her that it would be no problem, that when she would knew the exact date, time and details of the meeting, she could just let me know and I would be able to help her.

I provided her with the phone number of the agency that handled the bookings, told her that she had better let them know 24-48 hours in advance, if she wanted me to come, she simply had to provide the agency with my name, or else they would send another translator to meet her needs.

She took the agency's phone number that I had written down for her, put it in a small bag, and said goodbye with a gentle smile, touching my left shoulder with her right hand as a gesture of thanks.

It was early and Saturday, it was cold, very cold outside. As I walked down the stairs I could see a coffee shop, I had a hot coffee and, although I didn't like working on Saturdays, I thought that somehow I had helped someone to get an infection out of their body.

******

PA-01

A young man with a leg prosthesis (from the knee down). A case where the discussion, in inverted commas, comes from the existence of replacing the prosthesis. The mother insists on replacement, the DT does not understand the reason, and does not see enough arguments at the moment to replace it.

While the child hits the DT's table when moving, some objects fall on the floor, the mother repeats the same sentences assessing the need for replacement and I have to translate the same sentence again.

The mother stares at me, as if asking for the complicity in her request, as if she expects that with my translation the doctor will say: Yes, of course you have to replace it, and the DT avoids glances, submerging her face in her notes and medical history. She was also checking some things in a software, as she had the screen facing us (prosthesis stuff).

The mood was very cheerful, the boy took some sweets from his pocket, the mother changed her attitude almost at once and thanked the doctor for her help, as if she felt that the discussion was not the right one. I continued to do my task, standing up, and now, it was me who lowered my head.

The DT's room was small, most of the space was taken up by a huge desk, there was a window but it had translucent curtains, the room was lit with artificial light (I was shocked because it was two o'clock in the afternoon and the weather was nice, almost sunny).

The DT stood up again and checked the young man's leg, the upper part, the prosthesis was from before the knee downwards. He said that he could not find any infection, that everything was fine, that the annoyance they were talking about must have been for some other reason.

The boy laughed, I don't know why, and said things (in English), I thank him, because having to translate two people speaking at the same time is not that easy, I say this because the mother was talking non-stop, but the atmosphere was nice.

The doctor was laughing a lot now (I don't know why). The good thing about laughter is that it doesn't need to be translated. It's the best wild card for an IT.

It was all activity, lots of smiles, it didn't feel like a medical visit, and there didn't seem to be any signs of a physical impairment. If all consultations were like this, IT's mental health would never be compromised.

It was time to say goodbye, the conversation became slow and the doctor laughed, the young man and the mother returned the prothesis to its place of origin and headed for the door. The prothesis, seen from a distance, was invisible, that is, you could not guess that he was wearing it (it was covered by a pair of long and wide trousers).

The mother did not stop thanking me, which she did not translate because it was getting out of the door, she even put her hand on my shoulder as a gesture of gratitude, she did not stop laughing and so did the DT (don't ask me why, I have no idea).

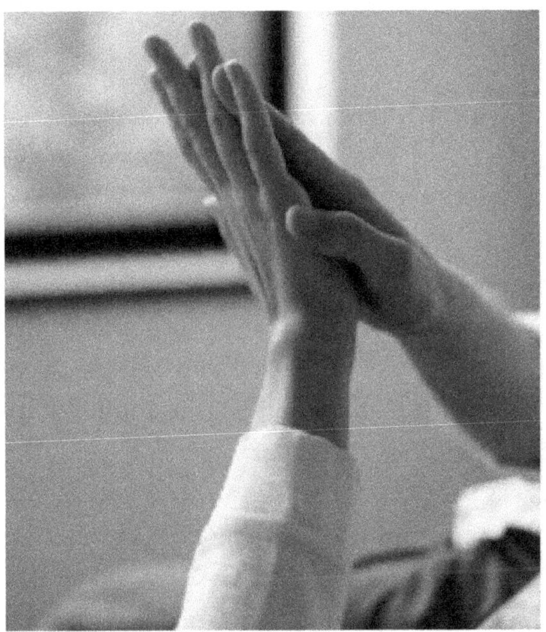

The DT requested me to wait a few moments, she would make some comments to me. She was hoping I could come back for the next session, for her to always have the same IT was more beneficial. She wanted to check if her way of expressing herself was good to facilitate the translation.

I thanked her for her questions (unusual in other meetings) and told her that her co-operation had been excellent. He had made my job easier and I felt that the PA was also satisfied with his support.

In this case there were clarifications. I also told her that she had introduced me correctly at the beginning of the session, mentioning that the IT was a non-clinical member of the healthcare team. All this had facilitated the degree of communication and trust. She smiled and spoke calmly.

******

PA-24.

This was an appointment with a psychologist, but it also included some medication, in particular a prick with a nurse, at the level of the abdomen. While she was receiving the prick from behind the curtain, she asked me to translate some questions, such as that she was in a lot of pain and some other things.

From what I could translate and deduce, given that it was a repetitive visit, the first time for me, she had suffered two miscarriages in a very short period of time and this had provoked some very serious health concerns. Hence the jab and other medication.

Her outward appearance was very good, she was about 35 years old, judging from my perspective and good looks, she spoke of the trouble to keep up her work and the struggle she had to make in this matter, which was crucial for her, as far as I could understand she had been alone since her arrival in the Middle.

She was addressing me very spontaneously, seeking to translate swiftly, one could say that she felt pretty confident in that aspect. They were now talking about some alleged previous reactions to a complication that had been discussed in the past, and how the pills were not working as well as expected. Now the punctures seemed to be going well.

The point is that today's jab was not expected to be in the abdomen, the PA-24 was grumbling so much, she almost didn't allow the DT to jab her. Finally, she agreed although she was telling me to interpret clearly that this process was too painful for her.

She was feeling very bad. They decided to adjourn the psychological consult, she was well enough for today with the needle prick. She would come back another day.

******

PA-73.

There were several families, most of them father and mother, others only the mother, I could not see any single father. I had been called to translate for a mother who was attending the meeting alone. There were no children.

I was not made aware of the topic or issues to be discussed. I was simply told the woman who was my PA and, I sat next to her, to interpret whatever was said.

The woman who was speaking had a high level of communication skills, I think that if she had set out to sell a property, a flat or anything else to those in the audience, I am sure she would have succeeded, everyone was paying her real attention, I would almost say astonishment. The atmosphere was very convivial.

We were all seated at a huge table. There were two women, who were in charge of the hospitality. One of them, as usual, mentioned in a generic way what was the reason for this meeting and what issues were going to be discussed.

To put it simply, we were dealing with Parent Coaching. It was not a one-off meeting, but several meetings over several weeks, one per week. The basic goal was to instruct the parents in detail on how to handle these children and to contrast the differing cases and behaviours, giving this information in a group, as in the management of a developmental therapy.

She commented that autism spectrum disorder (ASD) is a neurological and developmental disorder that affects the way people interact with others, communicate, learn and behave. Although autism can be diagnosed at any age, it is described as a "developmental disorder" because symptoms usually appear in the first 2 years of life.

I kept on translating the comments to my PA-73, which was next to me, albeit in a very low tone, without interfering with the meeting, as the others attending the meeting did not need IT, it was a simultaneous translation for one person only. In this case, my job was to make it easier for this mother to understand the meeting, because she did not ask any additional questions.

The topic of the meeting was a surprise, I had never before attended a meeting of parents of children who had been diagnosed with Autism. Now I knew what the meeting would be about.

As if that wasn't enough, he said that we were going to have a break of about 15 minutes. At the back he told us that there were drinks to refresh ourselves during the break. It was like a buffet, as IT I usually refuse to accept drink-food in the bookings, but today as it was all so familiar and with such a good atmosphere I decided to make an exception and, I went to the refreshment area.

There was a lot of selection, milk, coffee, assorted tea, ready-made sandwiches, pineapple and orange juices, assorted fruits, small croissants, ham, sliced cheese, coconut biscuits, chocolate biscuits and butter. It was really like a buffet breakfast in a fancy hotel.

Everyone present picked up the assorted foods and sat at the side tables to eat, not at the same table used for the meeting, another table at the back of the room. Despite the large number of people in attendance, there was plenty of space, which was appreciated. The atmosphere was so comfortable that we could have played Bingo and nothing would have happened.

It did not matter how much or how little each mother knew about the disease, they would all be supported in the same way.

Today, to start with, some specific behaviours of these children, which are typical in known cases, would be mentioned, then the parents present would be asked one by one if they have identified any of these behavioural patterns in their children, they would be asked to step in and express what they have seen (not forcing anyone).

This is a very empowering exercise, which helps parents to hear in person how other parents are in comparable reactions, that they are not alone and, at the same time, that they should be aware that their children are not "weirdoes".

Other basic points would be discussed. Some behaviours were cited, from several children, were certain patterns already identified as autistic behaviours, and parents were being asked to confirm that they had observed them at home (three nodded by a show of hands).

I assume that the speaker had a previous report from each of the families (from the way she expressed herself). This would be a test of behaviour and monitoring of those previous attitudes and practices that had already been referred to.

She addressed one of the mothers by name. Then, shecommented on some details he had noted about her son. She nodded in full agreement. The parent coaching programme focused on guiding parents to strategically promote their child's development through joyful interactions and activities that help address their child's unique needs.

It was based on the holistic approach of caregivers and natural supports in the child's life. Parents and caregivers know their children better than anyone else and these secure attachment relationships are vital in supporting children to develop and overcome challenges in this expressive and unique world of Autism.

DT: Too many professionals look at autism as something that needs to be controlled and contained. We look at autism as a neurodiversity that needs to be understood and the person needs to be supported in the right way. Once understood, then the person's potential can be realized. There are aspects of autism that are disabling and very challenging. Nevertheless, seeking to understand the neurodevelopmental differences in an effort to promote growth and development can help the autistic individual reach their potential while addressing the disabling aspects.

It was now giving four cases of children, following their family reports, showing the specific attitudes (four cases referred to):

Case 1. The child's presented symptoms are the result of underlying problems in the child's ability to perceive the world through his or her senses and use his or her body and thoughts to respond to it. These interfere with the child's ability to grow and learn, and lead to a diagnosis of autism.

Case 2. He showed hyper- or hyporeactivity to sensory input or unusual interest in sensory aspects of the environment (e.g. apparent indifference to pain/temperature, adverse response to specific sounds or textures, excessive smelling or touching of objects, visual fascination with lights or movement).

Case 3. Highly restricted, fixated interests that are abnormal in intensity or focus (e.g., strong attachment to or preoccupation with unusual objects, excessively circumscribed or perseverative interests).

Case 4. Deficits in nonverbal communicative behaviors used for social interaction, ranging, for example, from poorly integrated verbal and nonverbal communication; to abnormalities in eye contact and body language or deficits in understanding and use of gestures; to a total lack of facial expressions and nonverbal communication.

Whenever the DT referred to these connotations of different children, the other participants listened in total silence. There was a manifest interest in learning about variable situations of disorder, manifested in the families. It was as if by listening to each other's lack, they were preparing themselves for what might happen in the future to their own child.

Some think that children with autism cannot love with the same degree of warmth and intimacy as others. This is a false myth.

*****

PA-107.

The key word at this meeting was: medication, or more precisely, pills. It was a constant question and answer exchange, with PA-107 repeatedly urging for more pills.

I had previously encountered PA's who requested more pills, who were asking for more treatment or who demanded extra help from the DT, but I had never experienced such a curious and highly insistent case on the PA's part. It was genuine panic.

PA-107: I need more pills!.

Finally the DT agreed, giving a prescription, although different from the ones she already had.

Seeing that the name of the prescription did not match the previous medication, PA-107 went back on the attack. Now she did not hesitate to burst into tears. His displeasure was enormous.

The DT was solid and grave, unaffected by PA-107's whimpering. Translating when someone who is crying is tricky, the words come out choppy and it is not easy to discern the speech, even if they are short sentences that are uttered.

He recovered soon and was back to business. She wanted prescriptions for all the pills. How could she leave the previous ones?. What did that mean?.

On the way out, she told me that the DT was unbearable and unprofessional, that she was going to ask for a transfer. The next visit she would go to another DT even if she had to move to another part of town. We said goodbye without talking. I don't know if she would have the same opinion of me.

******

PA-90.

I had no background data on the patient, but I knew the Centre, it was always a mental health concern.

I was waiting for PA-90 to arrived, it didn't take long, there was no one there so I could identify her. She sat next to me, put her bag on the side of my chair.

The DT came out of her office, saw us and called me alone. It made me think that surely PA-90 wasn't pleased with my presence or that they might have decided to make a last minute change, but if she was going to call me alone, it wouldn't be a group issue.

She began to talk in a theoretical way about the work of the IT. She expressed herself in a very professional manner, saying things like:

Linguistic competence becomes more important as the degree of patient involvement increases, reaching its peak in encounters related to mental illness, behavioural and motivational issues, where nuances of meaning and subtleties of expression make the difference between shared understanding and total communication failure.

IT: Yes, of course, that's a crucial part of my job, arguably one of the motives that drives me to do this task of interpreting.

DT: I am an advocate for the use of IT in the NHS and the dominant model seems to be the use of agency interpreters on an ad hoc basis. This is an *ad hoc* nature of the assignment of interpreters, in this case face-to-face.

She paused, staring at me, so I nodded my head to indicate that I was following her reasoning.

IT: Of course, I know these matters from my training and official documents that I have reviewed several times. They are part of my preparation for this task.

DT: This issue helps in establishing a fruitful doctor-patient relationship and is key to effective practice management. The management of chronic diseases is greatly improved by continuity of care and the right linguistic support. I know very well that sometimes you also help with administrative tasks, making a very interesting collaborative work.

DT: I think you know the client, do you?. Because you know I have to make some checks, it is imperative that the psychologist identifies if there is a pre-existing non-professional relationship between the patient and the interpreter, for example, when the interpreter and the client have some history in common, such as having lived in the same community before emigrating.

If there is a greater likelihood of familiarity between the patient and the interpreter, there is a risk of a breach of confidentiality that may impact on the dynamics of communication, thus imposing barriers to open and honest dialogue.

IT: I can't say much about that, I live far from here, I accept bookings focused on other areas, very few here, I mean, I don't know the patient at all, I have no idea who she is, besides, as you can see in my file there are no personal details whatsoever, the agency does a very good job in that respect and is careful not to share personal details.

DT: Yes, I understand. The thing is that when you arrived, the PA sat next to you, and I got the impression that you were related. I even saw her put her bag on your chair.

She was seeing non-existent stuff, I had never seen this young woman in my life, I had never had any relationship with her and I had never had any booking with her in the past. Nothing at all.

DT: She has had a previous date with me, but hardly productive given her language limitations which I was unaware of at the time.

Clearly, finding limitations in the patient's English can greatly facilitate communication between PA-90 and the psychologist by working with a qualified interpreter to translate information from one language to another in an accurate, efficient and timely manner.

Including an interpreter in the psychological setting will be beneficial when the client prefers to speak, or speaks more fluently, in a language other than the psychologist's primary language, or when the client's English skills are deemed inadequate for the consultation.

IT: Of course, the language barrier must be eliminated in order to achieve a good service, I consider my work as fundamental in that task. I didn't really know what to think. On the one hand, the DT's explanations were very professional, she was clarifying basic aspects that I was grateful for, and she showed total acceptance of the use of IT's in this type of meeting.

But on the other hand, she left a doubt at the end of her comments, she didn't trust me to tell the honest thing, in a way she was giving me to assume that this PA-90 and I knew each other and that I wasn't telling the truth. This was starting to irritate me, although I kept my distance. I thought it was better to let her continue talking to see how far she would go with her arguments.

DT: As you know, there is a telephone IT option, but for me the face-to-face option is much more reliable and effective for my work. But of course, if you know the PA then this takes a back seat.

It was obvious, her mind had it all figured out. Whatever I said, her mind only accepted the option that PA-90 and I knew each other, it was not going to be easy to change her thoughts.

I decided not to argue with her, or try to refute her view, I simply thought I would listen to her comments, besides, she seemed to be a good psychologist, she expressed herself very competently, with professionalism.

My job was to fight and help with the translations, focusing on the communicational aspect, I couldn't get into an all-out argument first thing in the morning with a snooty psychologist who thought I knew PA-90 just because she had hung her bag on the same chair I was sitting in.

It could be that this programme is described in some Freudian or tabletop psychology workbook, I don't know, in my psyche and, in the context of the real situation, it was nothing more than a casual movement, just as she could have taken off the denim jacket she was wearing, or she could have hung her handbag on an empty chair, I don't even know if there were clothes hangers in the room, who knows! It was the first time I had seen that woman, that's for sure. Should I call a notary to validate that?.

I was trying to sort my mind in a constructive way to avoid any showdown. So I remembered the point of Interpersonal dynamics, set out in the agency and APS guidelines.

These guidelines were aimed at a problematic situation during translation, i.e. within a work meeting. How the IT could be expelled, but of course, in my case, right now, I was being judged before I started in a very non-convincing manner. Unless the PA has spoken to the DT, and told her something about me that I was unaware of. But at no time have I seen them together since my arrival.

She continued:

In this situation I am obliged to cancel the meeting, she said.

Then she said:

NHS National recommends that all British people should have the right to access services available free of charge to English-speaking British people, irrespective of their ethnic origin and mother tongue. Facilitating communication through interpreters is therefore important to ensure equitable and effective provision of psychological services.

I kept quiet, not wanting to incite any tension. She made it clear that I would be paid 100% of the booking. Should I thank her?.

I replied that I had understood her reasons and that I was going to leave because I would take the time to apply for another available booking in the area. I said goodbye as quickly and cordially as possible and went outside. On the way out, I could see PA-90 sitting in the same chair as when I had come in, checking her mobile phone.

She looked at me and waved, as if expecting me to come to her. Her bag was now between her legs, it looked like she had just taken her phone out of her bag. I thought the bag was nice, it was blue and medium in size.

I checked the attendance sheet signed by the DT. It said cancelled, with no additional comments. I thought it was inaccurate but, I was tired, I didn't feel like further messing around so I didn't make any extra comments for the agency, I just sent it back as it was with no further comments by me.

It would be really hard to explain to them that it was cancelled because PA-90 had the idea to hang her bag on the same chair I was sitting in. Even I find it hard to imagine, even though I was on the scene.

Summary

The interpreter will be able to negotiate both cultures at stake, those dependent on the languages involved. He can be neutral or active, or even form a bridge between the provider and the patient who does not speak the same language and who does not share the same view of things.

He can elaborate a transmission message based on equivalences, concepts and sufficient knowledge of the cultural context and background of the patient as well as of the medical culture. He will be able to struggle with and recognise the difficulty of the appropriate search for cultural equivalences.

And it will have to do so always ensuring the quality of interpretation under an authentic criterion in which there is no room for additional mediating functions.

In this way of approach he will define his primary function, the role of facilitator of the communication process between two people who do not speak the same language, in a dynamic of achieving the real goal of the encounter between the three, i.e. the patient's own well-being.

Facilitating the dialogue procedure requires much more than simple linguistic conversions, especially when the cultural framework of meaning for the patient and the provider are very different.

The interpreter not only achieves the appropriate linguistic conversion from one language to another, but also actively helps, where necessary, to overcome obstacles to communication arising from cultural, class, religious and other social differences.

The cases have been wide ranging, compelling, full of vibrancy and realism. Taken together they underpin the medico-social barriers to incremental intervention, where the lack of transparency, either in the terminology used or in the low-cut conceptualisations, makes it difficult for the parties to understand each other.

The narrative involves a large number of characters. Each of the patients who receive medical assistance, receiving at the same time verbal assistance.

These are characters immersed in a double struggle, on the one hand, to manage and deal with their ailments, and on the other, to obtain the communicative assistance that allows them to transmit their feelings and opinions with a total confidence that the receiver will comprehend them.

There are no struggles or tensions in this group, only collaboration and teamwork, even if it is within a reduced group of three components (PA + DT + IT).

The set of cases reported will lead us to the cultural imaginary of those who change countries, of those who need a social and linguistic recycling, of those who understand the word "culture" in their own way. Many cases are still up in the air. The closeness of the translation cannot go any further for the time being. I do not perceive the need for complete immersion in all the cases I have been able to assist.

The concretions between Psychologist, Interpreter and Patient, are emotions, doubts, a mechanism of hesitancy, placed between the projection of the medical care and the recreation of the patient who is trying to get better from his ailments. The interpreter remains in the shadows.

About the Author

Jorge Argibay holds a Master's degree in Comparative Literature from Autonoma University of Madrid, where he won the research award. This degree was combining with stays at the French University Paris-Diderot (Paris 7). He is a breath of contrasting knowledge in the field of interpretation, literary studies and the academic environment, with a touch of gentle lethargy.

He has extensive international experience and has immersed himself in the geography of countries as diverse as Mexico, Colombia, France, United Kingdom, China and the Philippines, in a constant quest to study other languages and cultural interactions. He has worked as an interpreter, teacher and researcher. He has applied his knowledge in the business world, by supporting multilingual teams in their task of recruiting new talent. His mind has been able to adapt to his obsession for travel itineraries, combining his admiration for other cultures, mixing it all in the same cocktail of his own destiny.